THE TEN COMMANDMENTS AND YOU

"Some morning from the boulder-broken beach
He would cry out on life, that what it wants
Is not its own love back in copy speech,
But counter-love, original response."

—Robert Frost, *The Most of It*

The Ten Commandments and You

by HAROLD EDWIN BERG

FORTRESS PRESS   ·   PHILADELPHIA

To Mildred

Table of Contents

Sinai Revisited

On the Sunday after President Kennedy's assassination in the fall of 1963 nearly every church in the United States recorded its largest attendance since the previous Easter. This tragedy had dramatized with classical clarity the neverending struggle between goodness and evil. Confronted by such unmistakable alternatives, the American people were in no doubt on which side to stand. They flocked to their churches in unprecedented numbers in an effort both to disassociate themselves from the wickedness which had brought down their President and to identify themselves with his inspired greatness. That a criminal act should drive them to church indicates that most people assume there is some connection between goodness and religion, yet few of them would be prepared to say what this relationship might be. In fact, there is a considerable amount of evidence that for the vast majority of Americans morality and religion have become separated, if not divorced, from one another.

In earlier, less complicated times, it was possible to take for granted that the good man was the religious man and the religious man the good man. Few people bothered to question this assumption even when they understood that there were irreligious men who were good and some religious men who were not. Now, however, it is not possible to make any automatic correlation between goodness and religion.

Widespread familiarity with psychology has enabled many people to realize how complicated human behavior is, and how many secret, unconscious motives a person may have for doing what he does. As popularly understood, much of psychology seems to suggest that a person may not be responsible for his actions, and that the adjectives "good" and "bad" have little meaning. According to this view, an act is neither good nor bad, but simply what a person does. One expression of this philosophy is the *Playboy* empire of Hugh Hefner. Capitalizing on the universal longing for more satisfying sexuality, the *Playboy* view of life promises to set men free, vicariously at least, by abolishing the traditional standards of sexual behavior. From this point of view, religion and moralism are the enemies of human happiness because they give a man a bad conscience, and his bad conscience inhibits his behavior. *Playboy* claims neither to encourage immorality (by which it means adultery) nor to condemn it, but simply to describe what is, or to be more precise, what men wish might be. But few of *Playboy*'s authors can afford to be so impartial, since the disappearance of adultery would leave them with nothing to write about. Thus they tend to glorify promiscuity with the same unconscious partiality with which Western movies lend glamor to murder and robbery.

Such supposed impartiality, however, does not solve this moral dilemma; it only evades it. However determined modern man may be to refrain from passing judgement on human behavior and to erase the distinctions between good and evil, these categories keep reasserting themselves in the most unlikely places. The constant claim to moral objectivity and the repeated desire for suspended judgement are themselves mute evidence that men do unconsciously tend to evaluate their actions. They may postpone, but they cannot forever avoid the need for drawing lines between good and bad, for making judgements which are independent of prevailing opinion.

Another factor of modern life which has called into question the relationship between goodness and religion is the apparent failure of the traditional sources of morality to influence human behavior. Religion in general and the Ten Commandments in particular have usually been considered the basis for moral conduct. Among Christians there has been general agreement that God intended the Ten Commandments to serve as rules for human behavior, and that goodness consists in a strenuous effort to conform to them. Thus, as the propagator of the Decalogue, the church has long been regarded as the creator and defender of morality. But

the much vaunted "return to religion" which is supposed
to have taken place in the United States following
World War II has had no observable effect either on
public or on private morality. Church membership and
the rate of crime, for example, are each now at their
highest levels in American history. And so far as human
rights are concerned, some of the most zealous crusaders
for social justice in this century have disavowed any
connection with religion, while the church has been
among the slowest of contemporary power structures to
respond to the demand for racial equality.

Valiant efforts have been made to bridge this gap
between goodness and religion. Moral preachment has
been the church's stock in trade for most of this century, and the sermon has become a kind of ethical pep
talk, the congregation being urged Sunday after Sunday
to "live its religion on Monday morning." The faithful
are given rather explicit directions as to how this may
be done: they are to pray, worship, give, build, con-
tribute, attend, go, witness, to which may be added all
the other imperative verbs which describe an "active"
religion. But when modern man appears not to be listening, or if listening, not conforming, the preacher's frus-
tration is likely to lead to scolding as he assumes the
role of the denouncing prophet. While such "laying
down the law" may, to be sure, produce a few bad
consciences, it does not offer much creative guidance to
people caught in difficult and subtle ethical dilemmas.
Still less does it suggest how their morality is to flow
out of their life with God. For the average person there

is simply no connection between his religion and his goodness. Perhaps the commonest expression of this moral crisis is the remark, "I can be good without going to church." For most people this is exactly so.

In the face of this situation, the claim of this book is that if modern morality is no longer shaped by religion, this is not because the Ten Commandments are obsolete, but because they have been misunderstood and therefore wrongly used. The Ten Commandments have usually been regarded as ethical principles which can be imposed without reference to God. This separation between the commandments and God has contributed heavily to the divorce between goodness and religion. The Ten Commandments must therefore be reconsidered to see how they relate to man's life with God.

The Decalogue stands at the center of the Old Testament's second book. While this book is called Exodus in its English translations, less than half its material deals with Israel's departure from Egypt. The larger part of the book concerns itself with the founding and ordering of Israel's life as a nation. Like the four other books which with Exodus make up the Books of the Law, Exodus is a rather late edition of at least four earlier written and oral traditions, and is to be regarded not so much as a history of Israel as an interpretation of that history. We must see the book as a sixth-century B.C. challenge to a people struggling to reestablish themselves as a nation after their long exile in Babylon.

Exodus declares that the meaning of Israel's separate

existence as a nation is to be found in God's revelation of himself as the redeemer and rescuer of his people. Just as God had once called Abraham from his homeland to a strange new land and then had made a covenant with him, so at the Exodus God first brought about the release of the enslaved Israelites, and then reestablished the covenant with them. The heart of this covenant was God's promise that this new nation was to be his special possession and instrument. This promise grew out of God's gift of deliverance and depended for its fulfillment on the faithfulness and grateful obedience of Israel. The Exodus came before the Ten Commandments. This sequence is important. First God redeems, then he demands. And the answer to this demand is called forth from the rescued by the very nature of the rescuer.

The actual origin of the Ten Commandments is lost in antiquity. How much of the law contained in Exodus may actually be attributed to Moses himself is uncertain. Many sections of the Exodus legislation, as well as that which is to be found in the other books of Moses, originated in the so-called Deuteronomic period, that is, during the time after the sixth-century exile when these books were given their present form. Whatever may have been the actual origin of the Ten Commandments, however, the authors and later editors of Exodus clearly saw them as the heart of the covenant relationship between Israel and God. The Decalogue is a kind of "Bill of Rights" from which all other Hebrew legislation flows, just as our own Bill of Rights is basic to the Constitution of which it is a part, even though in point of time it came as something of an afterthought. If, as some scholars believe, the Ten Commandments were formulated somewhat later than the earliest laws of Moses, they are still basic to them. The actual commandments are not workable laws in themselves, cast as they are for the most part in the negative, but rather serve to provide the climate in which legislation may be formulated and obeyed.

This distinction between the Ten Commandments and all other Hebrew law is to be seen in the Exodus narrative which surrounds them. Unlike later legislation which is said to have been given to Moses alone, the Ten Commandments were given with the entire nation standing at respectful attention at the foot of the mountain within sight of God's smoke and sound of his thunder. Accompanying this handing down of the Decalogue are all the traditional Hebrew symbols for holiness: ritual purification, trumpets, fire, thunder, lightning, and earthquake. In every other instance in the scriptures where these elements appear in any combination, they underscore the authentic presence of God. Here also, Exodus makes it clear that the Ten Commandments have to do primarily with God, and only secondarily with man.

Most revealing is the narrative concerning the second giving of the Decalogue (Exod. 32ff.). Moses disappeared for so long a time the people concluded that he had abandoned them or that he had died up on the mountain. In either case, to a primitive people only recently released from generations of slavery and sur-

rounded for centuries by Egyptian gods, the loss of
Moses would mean the loss of God. Aaron assumed
leadership in the absence of his brother and acceded to
the nation's longing for a visible god by fashioning a
golden calf similar to the gods they had seen in Egypt.
Thus in the wilderness they were comforted by one
reminder of the life they had left behind and were
already beginning to long for. The anger of Moses when
he returned to find them involved in pagan ritual drove
him to break the stone tablets of the law, suggesting
that Moses himself at first misunderstood the meaning
of the Decalogue. He took it to be a description of ideal
human behavior and when he saw how far removed
from reality it was, he destroyed it.

Later, when the golden calf had been removed and
the people admonished for their apostasy, Moses was
moved to ask for a vision of God. The answer to his
plea for a glimpse of God's face was a second copy of
the Ten Commandments. Moses hid in the cleft of a
rock to watch God's glory passing by, and his vision,
when he had reduced it to scratches in stone, became
the Decalogue. The Ten Commandments are not about
man. They are about God. This explains why the stone
tablets were placed within the Ark of the Covenant
which was kept in the Holy of Holies and made central
to all Hebrew worship. The presence of the law was
the presence of God.

A clue to the proper understanding of the Decalogue
is to be found in Psalm 119. Again and again the long
psalm asserts, "O how I love thy law." On first reading,

such a phrase sounds like pious nonsense. Nobody *loves* the law. The law is to be obeyed, not loved. We would think a person unbalanced to be so enamored of the law as to spend all his waking time thinking about it. This is because we associate this law with human rules and regulations which are never especially lovable. But if God himself is hidden in the law, then the law can be loved because it is a picture, not of man, either as he is or ought to be, but of God, both what he does and what he promises to do.

God never asks a man to do something for him without first doing something for that man. Indeed, there is nothing anyone can do for God which God does not make possible by his prior grace. Jesus indicates in the Sermon on the Mount that obedience to the law is made possible when salvation is known to be present, and that he himself came not to eliminate the law but to fulfill it, that is, to give flesh and blood reality to the promises implied by the law. The Beatitudes are to the Sermon on the Mount what the Ten Commandments are to the law of Moses. For on close examination, the Beatitudes turn out to be a marvelous description of Christ himself. Both the Beatitudes and the Ten Commandments are delineations, not of man, but of God, and his incarnate Son, the obedient, Suffering Servant. Neither the Old Testament nor the New anywhere suggests that moral law is a principle of behavior which may be separated from its source and applied objectively in any human situation. The Bible simply does not think in terms of conformity to principles. It speaks rather of response to the God who lives and acts, who moves now in one place, then in another, now at one moment, then at another. Such a God cannot be confined within predictable principles of behavior, nor can response to him be reduced to rules and regulations which can always and everywhere be impartially enforced. The only adequate response to such a God is love.

But to turn men loose with the vague directive that they love God and one another is to imply that love is formless and unstructured. Such an implication does violence to the central affirmation of the Christian faith, that the Word was made flesh. Flesh has shape and structure. The incarnation identifies and defines a particular man at a particular moment in history. No one can encounter a God of such concreteness without reacting in equally three-dimensional terms. A vague, spiritualized God inspires only vague religious feelings. He can be loved with an interior, invisible love. But the God of the Bible has spelled out his love in historic activities. The only adequate response to such love is an equally historic performance, and to be historic, love must occupy time and space. There is no love apart from the acts of love. Christian love is not responsibility to a lifeless code; it is response to a living, eternal personality. Precisely because this personality is hidden within the law, response to him will be a reply in time and space, an answer of ordered obedience.

Where the commandments are seen to be merely ideal ethical principles, there man confronts a schizophrenic God; the "angry" God of the Old Testament who is to

be feared and obeyed, the God who once moved and
acted in history, has been supplanted by the sweet and
gentle Jesus of the New Testament, the God who is to be
loved and adored but who is powerless to move within
society and across history except as he is able now and
then to inspire noble sentiments in men. This explains
why modern man thinks of God in the Old Testament
in terms of his "anger" and his holiness and in the New
Testament in terms of his love, yet he cannot think of
holiness as lovable nor of love as holy. He cannot both
fear and love God at the same time, as he is instructed
to do by the catechism. In fact, it strikes him as a
contradiction in terms to speak of both fearing and
loving the same God. Thus goodness and religion part
company because goodness is supposed to be conformity
to an ethical norm while religion is supposed to be
"spiritual" response to a vapid, spiritualized God. Men
soon tire of such dull conformity and such vague, irrele-
vant religion.

Most Americans would probably describe the United
States as a "God-fearing" nation, and would point to the
furor over the unconstitutionality of directed prayers
in the public schools as a case in point. But Americans
tend also to be unconcerned about basic human rights,
as reflected in the vast amount of opposition or indif-
ference to racial equality. This unconcern indicates that
our fear of God may well be unrelated to human relationships and attitudes. Public morality, therefore, tends
to be determined by the consensus of accepted public
opinion, and is thus prevented from being a response

to the God of the law. Since goodness does not create
society, society creates goodness. A man is good not for
his neighbor's sake but for his own, since he can become
a part of his society only by conforming to it and by
subscribing to its prevailing notion of goodness.

The individual is thus drawn into society not by his concern for it, but by his fear of risking its disapproval. His
"goodness" becomes his attempt to win his neighbor's approval in much the same way as his display of the currently
accepted status symbols establishes his importance. His
greatest fear is that he will not be accepted; his greatest
punishment is rejection. The individual demonstrates by
his behavior that he belongs. The desire to be accepted,
either by God or by other men, is the principal motive for
goodness whenever goodness does not grow out of faith,
because faith is the knowledge that one has already been
accepted. Without this knowledge of acceptance, goodness degenerates into a mere attempt to win approval.

In our society any behavior which does not conform
to the current notion of goodness is regarded as immoral.
The cult of the beatniks, now pretty well domesticated,
was not so much a revolt against morality as it was a
revolt against a society which presumes to decide for
men what is good and what is bad. The beatnik cultus
collapsed when it was rather gleefully pointed out that
the beats were also conformists in their own fashion,
imitating rather than revolting against the society of
which they were so critical. Nevertheless, the beatniks
were very right in showing that the self-made society
may become quite immoral without ever being aware

of this, since to criticize the accepted, established norms is to invite almost certain reprisal. To criticize such a society is to threaten its very existence and so to risk being classified as a subversive. This kind of society will inevitably claim divine sanction for its morality, and see itself as being based upon the immutable law of God, and therefore no room for dissent or difference is possible. The usefulness of God, who is invoked on every public occasion at which his presence does not prove embarrassing, is that he maintains the world just as it is. Seldom does the moral conformist recognize that his goodness is really without foundation, and is therefore incapable of relating him either to God or to another human being, but is, in fact, an effective barrier to genuine communication with God and man. The separation between goodness and religion produces sterile, imprisoning morality as well as stuffy religion.

This separation exists because the Ten Commandments have been reduced to moral principles of ethical human behavior. To reconsider the Ten Commandments in their context is to see them not as rules and regulations, but as an image of the hidden God, who has given us the law so that we might respond to him in spontaneous, unpredictable, three-dimensional reality. The God who commands is the God who redeems, the God of victorious self-giving who hides himself within those human needs which cry out at us from beside the thoroughfares of an everyday world made holy by the knowledge of his love and made loving by the knowledge of his holiness.

2

The Eternal Companion

"I am the Lord your God, who brought you out of the land of Egypt, out of the house of bondage. You shall have no other gods before me."

—*Exodus* 20:2-3

One of the profound insights of Genesis is that "it is not good that man should be alone." Yet loneliness is virtually forced upon man in the modern world in his solitary struggle to compete for and win approval and acceptance from his fellowmen. The alarming population explosion of our time has created a loss of privacy without resulting in an end to loneliness. In fact, the crowded city tends to heighten loneliness, since the sight of so many strangers, each going his own way, none of them concerned about or even aware of the existence of the lonely one, only reinforces basic isolation.

This loneliness, however, has nothing to do with aloneness, which is quite another matter. Aloneless is also, to be sure, a modern problem. One of the very real obstacles to polar and spacial exploration is the haunting fear of vast aloneness at the frozen places of the world or in the infinities of outer space. One can hardly conceive of the hunger for the sound of another human voice which would build up in a man hurtling light years away from the place of his birth. Yet such physical and astronomical aloneness can be tolerated by a person of sufficient strength and stability. It is, rather, the utter immediacy of myriad lives—say, in a crowded housing development—which brings loneliness to the breaking point. *Here* is community without communion, conversation without communication, company without companionship.

The word companion has its origin in Latin, where it meant one who breaks bread with another. At meal time, when there is a lull in the day's activities and a moment for reflection, there comes a hunger for more than food. There is a longing for someone to reach out to, to talk with, to break bread with. We never really see ourselves except by reflection in the response of another human being. Lacking such a responsive companion, man is locked inside the shell of his own loneliness.

If there were nothing more to loneliness than this, it would, for most people, be a relatively easy problem to solve. The world does not lack for companionable people, each of them also seeking sympathetic understanding. On the surface it seems quite easy for a man simply to reach out and relate himself to someone else. That he does not often do so suggests that while he fears loneliness, he fears love even more. He holds back partly out of fear that he will be rejected, and also partly out of fear that he may be received too well, that he will be loved more than he is prepared to love, that he will become so involved in another person's life that he will lose something of his own freedom and individuality.

If human love is or can be so frightening a thing, how terrifying is the love of God! Little wonder that in the face of so overpowering a love, man is tempted to domesticate God's love, to reduce it to manageable proportions, to substitute for an eternally active personality a static mental image, a noble but unthreatening ideal which can be worshipped without commitment. Nowhere is this unconscious reduction of God to be seen more clearly than in the popular understanding of the Ten Commandments. Because man's first instinct is to preserve his own independence, and because the Ten Commandments seem to be designed expressly to hem him in, he tends to reduce the Decalogue to the lowest common denominator of obligation.

As an example of this, the first commandment is taken to mean little more than a prohibition against worshipping stone images, and since the impulse to pray to carved deities does not rank high on the list of today's irresistible temptations, this command can be all but written off as a meaningful guide for life in modern times. The second command appears to involve only a slight change in one's vocabulary, and the third a minor distraction in one's weekly schedule. Such requirements can easily be met and as easily forgotten. But in this process of reducing the commandments to their minimum, God is also reduced, since a God with small demands is a small God. And a small God cannot command a large allegiance.

But neither is a small God adequate to assist a man through the complexities of life. So, having deflated the real God to manageable proportions, man finds it necessary to construct other gods, ideal images for these emergency situations and those ultimate questions which cannot finally be avoided. The first commandment has to do with this very matter of inventing gods and of plural gods.

There is an irony in the narrative surrounding the Ten Commandments. While Moses was receiving the first commandment on the top of Mount Sinai, the Israelites down below were breaking it. They brought their gold jewelry and trinkets to Aaron so that he could make them a golden calf. Unwilling to submit to the strenuous expectations of the God of Moses, but unable to face the wilderness alone, they created their own god. They discovered what men have always known: that everyone must have a god even if he must invent one of his own.

Man is never more inventive than when he is creating gods to worship. He does this so easily that he is hardly conscious of it. He is conscious only of an overwhelmingly mysterious world with which he cannot always cope. Yet in his reluctance to admit that he may not be the sole master of his fate, he searches for some acceptable symbol of authority which will sustain him in his need but not rob him of his own sense of mastery. Worship something he will and he must. But how much easier and more comfortable it is to worship a god he has himself created, a god he can see, a god who will demand nothing more of him than that he worship. On close examination, every man-made god turns out to be an extension of the man who worships it. It is either the objectification of the most ideal and perfect thing he can imagine, that which fills him with the greatest pride and satisfaction, or it is the symbol of all that he fears, as if by making his terror visible he might control and master it. In either case, man-made gods do not and cannot change men. It is men who create such gods after their own image so that they can feel safe and comfortable with them. No one can be comfortable in the presence of such overwhelming love as God has shown. Such love is infinitely terrifying and vastly threatening. How much easier to retreat from it and in the silence of one's own loneliness construct and worship a more manageable, less frightening god.

"We should fear and love God," Luther says in his catechism. This is, to be sure, a particular kind of fear, expressed in such words as "awe" or "dread" or "holiness." It is the trembling we have felt in the presence of majestic beauty, the Grand Canyon, perhaps, or the giant redwoods of northern California, Brahms's First Symphony or Bach's B Minor Mass, the Sistine Chapel or the Chartres Cathedral, El Greco's "View of Toledo" or the poetry of William Blake. This is a fear which sweeps us along by sheer contagion. If this is fear at all in the ordinary sense, it is the fear that we might be left behind, that somewhere in the universe there is a joy and a beauty which we might never know, which we could not bear to miss. Something stirs deep within us, a primitive hunger for God which makes him seem the

most obvious and inevitable fact of our existence, like a
new experience which seems suddenly and strangely
familiar, as if remembered from another life. This is the
feeling we have in the presence of all great art. It seems so
right, so natural, like music which is unbearably beautiful
and so perfect that it almost seems that we might have
written it ourselves, or else that no one really wrote it
because it must always have been so, waiting, perhaps,
only for someone to hear it and put it down on paper.
We can sense nothing of the agony of its creation, only
the composer could know that. Even so when we
encounter God; it seems to us that we have always
known him, that he is just as we imagined he would be,
that we could not improve on him had we fashioned him
ourselves, and yet we did not. And this is what over-
whelms and frightens us, that he is there, waiting for us
to hear and see him, as though we had emerged from
a long, dark corridor to find ourselves suddenly in some
vast cathedral.

There is such tension, such agony in our relationship
with God as may be found in any genuine love affair.
We say sometimes, only half seriously, that we cannot
live with or without our love. God is like that. Our
temptation, as it has been for all humanity, is to resolve
the tension, to ease the agony, by making God over in
our image, by inventing a substitute god of our own in
whose presence we can worship and whose power we
can trust without being made to feel uncomfortable.

In the face of this, however, we are told: "I am the
Lord your God. You shall have no other gods beside

me." And our first thought is to say, "Well, if there are no other gods, then how can we have any other gods?" Of course, any other god would have to be a synthetic one who will let us down just when we need him most. But this has never prevented men from finding all sorts of quite respectable things to trust in and to worship. We could not endure to live for long in the unrelenting honesty of God's actual presence, and so we seek out more comfortable houses of worship where our lesser gods will leave us as we are. And if the shrines to such gods can be brought into the house of the Lord, so much the better. Then the illusion is complete. Every god of human creation is designed to make a man feel good without disturbing him. A man who can relax at worship is worshipping a false god, especially if that worship happens in a church. There are more pantheons called churches than strict Christian monotheism would care to admit. Here is where success, power, wealth, popularity, lust, pleasure, and security are worshipped like the ancient golden calf, the powerless, meaningless, pathetic substitutes for God.

"We should fear, love and trust in God above all things," the catechism teaches us to say. How clear and obvious this is. And yet, how difficult, perhaps impossible, it is. Here is the agony, here is the central struggle of every human life, the effort to break through the barriers of silence to an eternal companionship which will not rob us of our own true destiny. In spite of the difficulty of this struggle, we must resist every temptation to resolve the agony by settling for a god who is less than real. No one who thought that he might one day see the living God could ever be contented with a puny little god of his own creation, a god he could encounter and manipulate without fear. The tragedy for those who disobey this commandment is that they have their god, for all the good this does them. In the hour of their need, in the moment of their death, let them call on their golden calf, their sports car, their gracious home, their shelf of trophies, their bank account, their press clippings, all the things to which they have devoted their first allegiance, and let them lie waiting for an answer.

Those who keep this commandment will know agony. They will be tortured by their hunger for a God who hides himself, a God who is beyond all possessing, all demonstration and proof. And as they grow closer to him in living response, they will also be made aware of their own inadequacy, so that their agony grows, the nearer they are to God, like a dissonance which grows slowly more unbearable as the notes come closer together. But as a dissonance demands resolution, so God commands a living response. We can resist him only for awhile, and then we must either come to him or ourselves become as non-existent as the gods we have worshipped.

"You shall have no other gods." This is as much a promise as it is a demand. God is here assuring us that though we can have no other god, we will always have him.

3

What's in a Name?

*"You shall not take the name of The Lord your God
in vain; for the Lord will not hold him guiltless who
takes his name in vain."*

—*Exodus 20:7*

People's names were considered far more important in
ancient times than they are today. Nowadays there may
be a momentary debate at the birth of a child when
parents look through lists of names in an attempt to find
one which strikes their fancy, but when the name has
been selected and recorded, it is no longer taken very
seriously. We are inclined to ask with Shakespeare
"What's in a name? That which we call a rose by any
other name would smell as sweet."

Yet not always so. People once took names more
seriously, because there was once the feeling that a
person's name was a part of himself. This explains the
great care with which John the Baptist and Jesus were
named. Already implied in the names given to them by
the angel were their character and their destiny. All
Hebrew names have a meaning—Jesus means "Strong
Deliverer." No one could speak the name of the Savior

without being reminded of his ministry. This must even have been so for Jesus himself. Each time he heard or spoke his own name, he was reminded of who he was. Jesus' name recalled him again and again to his God-given destiny, almost as if, having been given such a name, he was obliged to fulfill its meaning. In this sense his name was indeed a part of him. Our Lord might have been named anything at all, and perhaps this would have made no difference in his character—certainly there were many other men whose name was the same as his—but people tend somehow to live up to what is expected of them, and for Jesus a part of this great expectation was contained in his name.

Very few people are entirely satisfied with the names which their parents chose for them even though they seldom go to the trouble of making changes. Still, if it were for them to do, few people would choose the names they have for there is more to this name dropping than is first apparent. It reflects a person's unconscious underlying dissatisfaction with himself, and suggests that if he changed his name he might somehow also bring about a change within himself. The stage names used by most actors, movie stars, and singers reveal this search for a new identity. Very few such celebrities have become famous under their own names. In fact, many of these personalities are wholly the products of their press agents, living fan magazine existences which have litttle basis in reality. The allure of their names becomes a box office attraction. The world hangs breathlessly on the news of their latest infidelities, and is shocked to dis-

cover at their death that they were only human beings
after all with their own burdens and private griefs.

This feeling that a name is part of the person who
bears it explains the gravestones in the cemetery. These
markers are relics from more superstitious times when
it was thought that a man's eternity depended on the
perpetuation of his name. We still tend to imagine that
if a person's name is engraved indelibly in indestructible
stone, then the person himself has not yet passed into
oblivion, but if his name should be forgotten, then it
would almost be as if he had never existed. This sense
of the importance of names is also reflected in our word
for baptism. We sometimes call this sacrament "christen-
ing," that is, the giving of a person's Christian name.
In ancient times when a person was converted and
baptized, he took a new name. Similarly with biblical
personalities. Abraham and Paul were both given new
names by God by way of dramatizing the revolutionary
change which had taken place in them.

Due to the importance which men attached to a
person's name, and their feeling that a name was itself
a part of the person, the ancient Hebrew had a regard
for the name of his God which was not less than his
regard for God himself. Misuse or careless use of God's
name could only reflect disregard for God. To abuse
the name of God was the equivalent of attacking God
himself, a prospect so terrifying that the Jew was
reluctant to use the name at all, feeling perhaps that it
was better not to say his name than to run the risk of
taking it in vain.

I can remember that when I was a boy our family acquired a much needed new dining room set, the most beautiful feature of which was the marvelously smooth and shiny table top. Such perfection must, of course, be protected in a large and active family, and so my mother, meticulous housekeeper that she was, covered it immediately. When not in use, the table top had to be protected, and when it was in use, it had also to be protected. As a result of all this safeguarding, we never saw that lovely table top again. Now what is the good of beauty which cannot be seen? And what is the good of a name which cannot be used? (To fail to use God's name is also a kind of disrespect.) One can be as careless about God's name by using it too seldom as by using it in improper ways.

When we hear or think of the commandment, "You shall not take the name of the Lord your God in vain," we think automatically about swearing. God's name gets used in a lot of ways which are not exactly theological. This happens so unconsciously and so unintentionally that a person may well be unaware of it. He may even excuse himself on this ground, by saying that he wasn't thinking and so didn't really mean what he said. Well, this is precisely one meaning of the phrase "in vain." If someone says, "They tried to save the child but their efforts were in vain," you know exactly what is meant. Their efforts were useless and to no avail. To use God's name pointlessly is in a way more serious than to swear knowingly and purposely. For this is to put God's name in the same category as any other casual word of con-

versation. It is to make God's name common and trivial.
When most people curse they have no idea what they
have said. When someone says, "God damn you," he is
really saying, "May God condemn you," and this is a
form of prayer. If a person were to mean this, it would
imply that he believed God had the ability to condemn
people, and that God would do so if through such a
curse he were asked. This is less to be deplored than to
use the same words as if they had no more meaning
than "my dog has fleas."

The careless, casual, crude way in which people who
know better use God's name indicates that there is for
them no sense of the reality, the power, or holiness of
God. God has become for them trivial and common-
place. What they need is not a lesson in cultivated conversation but an experience of God's reality and presence. The second commandment is not urging us to
greater fussiness in the way we talk; it is confronting us
with the reality of God. For God cannot be separated
from his name. There is, to be sure, a relationship between how a person feels about God and how he uses
God's name in conversation, but one dare not for a
moment suppose that he has fulfilled this command simply by changing his vocabulary. We so often give the
world to believe that the difference between a Christian
and a non-Christian, in terms of the second commandment, is a matter of the choice of words. Nothing could
be farther from the real heart of the matter. A man's
speech might be salty and his heart warm toward God,
while another might have immaculate, sanitary speech

and a heart which is cold and aloof. This is not to excuse carelessness. One who is sensitive and aware of the presence of God will be only too painfully aware how far short all his conversation falls in reflecting adequately his own dependence and indebtedness to God. He needs no more to be reminded about careless use of God's name than a son must be told that he ought not take his mother's name in vain, or a lover that he ought not swear falsely by the name of his beloved.

An ironical fact, however, is that those persons most busy about the things of religion are very often those most tempted to take God's name in vain. Those most in danger are those whose lives are so close to the church and so filled with religious activities that sacred things are often handled with careless familiarity, God and godly affairs deprived of their holiness, and the name of God rolled off the tongue as if it were any other three-letter word.

There are two ways by which communication between God and man breaks down. It happens when men stop calling on God. And it happens when they call on him so casually that they might as well be talking to themselves. In either case, something so essential has been lost that the whole meaning and purpose of human life is radically altered. When God is trivialized and reduced to an expression of speech, he is no longer a power to be reckoned with. Man is left with no one to turn to, no one to call on, no one outside himself to believe in beyond the little gods which are extensions of himself. Nothing could be lonelier or more terrifying than a life devoid of communication with God, a life closed in on every side by the dimensions of the self, a life in which the vastness of the universe gives back no other answer than the empty echo of our own cry for help. The most priceless possession we have, the gift which more than any other transforms our life, the key which unbars a life locked in between the cradle and the grave and throws it open to eternity, that key is the name of God. Without it, we are powerless. With it, the power of God is ours. The Almighty has given us his name. He has asked us, indeed, he has begged us, to call on him. And what is more, he has promised to hear and to answer us.

We are not talking now about vocabulary. We are talking about communication, our conversation with God, the heart of our spiritual life. The command is a summons to us to take stock of our interior life. It is a reminder that all human communication begins from the inside, that it is our hearts, not our tongues, which need to be tidied. The tragedy is that we are too apt to wait until crisis or catastrophe before we speak with God. But God is no unfeeling stone who hears us only when the walls collapse around us. God is love, which means that he is hungry for the sound of our voice; he wants to hear us speak his name, else why did he go to such pains to give it to us, and why does he struggle so through all the years of history to keep that name alive, revealing himself afresh to each new generation?

To live in such a state of constant communication with God requires of us an openness to him. To the extent that we lack such openness and want to hide from God, our love cannot grow and our prayers are in constant danger of becoming empty words and meaningless phrases. There is perhaps no greater taking in vain than that which occurs in the kind of hasty, thoughtless recitation of formal prayers which is a caricature of conversation with the living God. This fact ought to give pause to those who would require men to pray by law. No doubt it happens to us all that our minds wander while we pray. How easily we turn to the children or the weather or the crucial appointment on Monday morning during those long prayers on Sunday when the pastor covers so much territory before he gets around to us and our needs. It is more important to discipline our minds than to curb our tongues. Only so will God become a reality for us, and only so will our prayers become genuine, responsive conversation with the living God. When this happens, then this commandment, like the first, becomes a promise. "You shall not take the name of the Lord your God in vain," can also mean, "You will never speak my name to no avail. I will always hear. For I am the Lord your God."

"O Lord, our Lord, how majestic is thy name in all the earth!"

4

Every Day's a Holy Day

> "Remember the sabbath day, to keep it holy. Six days
> you shall labor, and do all your work; but the seventh
> day is a sabbath to the Lord your God; in it you shall
> not to do any work, you, or your son, or your daughter,
> your manservant or your maidservant, or your cattle, or
> the sojourner who is within your gates; for in six days
> the Lord made heaven and earth, the sea, and all that
> is in them, and rested the seventh day; therefore the
> Lord blessed the sabbath day and hallowed it."
> —*Exodus 20:8-11*

The commandment on keeping the Sabbath challenges
us to build a fixed and calculated routine for God within
the framework of our living. It carefully provides regular
access for God into our activities, a structured schedule
which will reflect our own eagerness to meet him and
which will declare to the world the reality of his being.

There was a time, when the church was young, when
few Christians had any day of rest at all. For most of
them one day was like another; the only worship they
had was at secret services in out-of-the-way places which
were hid from the rest of the world. As soon as they
could arrange it, however, they provided for a holy

day, and for them this was to be the first day of the
week, the day of resurrection. Perhaps the early Christians intentionally abandoned the seventh day as if to
make a clear break from their Jewish origins, or perhaps
they saw that more than a day of the week is at stake
in the keeping of this commandment.

As it stands in Exodus, this commandment says nothing
at all about *worshipping* on the seventh day. It says
simply that a man is to take one day of rest every
seventh day. He is to guard this day and keep it from
becoming just another day of the week. He is to insist
upon this not only for himself, but for everyone else in
his family and household, including guests and livestock.

It is important to see that there is here no medical
or psychological rationale for the need of human beings
for rest and relaxation. Rather, the command grows out
of the creative activity of God. If—in the picture
language of Genesis 1—even God finally came to an
end of his work, who is man that he should work on and
on as if to outdo and outdistance God? Seen in this
perspective, the command serves to keep us in our
proper relationship with reality. We are creatures. The
unresting man who rushes from one business appointment to another, whose days and nights fade into one
another in an unending flurry of activity, is trying in one
way or another to build his own little empire, to shoulder
a larger burden of the world's responsibility than a mere
man is entitled to. So long as he keeps going, he can
convince himself that perhaps he is some sort of god
after all. But let him stop, let him rest for a whole day

within the quiet bosom of his family, and he will soon
be cut down to size again. Let him stay at home one
day to help with the dishes and entertain the guests
and put the children to bed and he will soon be divested
of any illusions of divinity.

Even though this commandment says nothing at all
about worship, its relationship to worship was seen long
before the Christian era. This came about not because of
the words "sabbath" and "holy," which here refer only to
a day of rest kept apart, but because of the liturgical
allusion to the six days of creation. Every remembrance
of creation was for the Jew an opportunity to praise the
Creator. So on the first day of the week, God was to be
praised for his creation of light; on the second day,
for his creation of the earth; on the third, for the fruits
of the earth. The creation account was a devotional
guide, culminating in a day on which God heard the
sounds of praise from his creation, and man devoted
himself to the important business of worship and
thanksgiving.

This would explain how knowledge of God's great act
of creation was kept alive in those prehistoric days
before men learned to write. The fact of creation was
woven into the fabric of their lives, so that every day
was a reminder of it, and every day of rest an opportunity to tell and retell that marvelous story about when
the world was new and man was innocent and God
could be seen walking across the woodlands and waste-
lands of the world. Even now, after so many millenia,
there is a charm and freshness about the creation story

which never fails to grip and move us. Men could not have kept this story alive unless they had had an opportunity and a reason for telling it over and over again, until it was indelibly inscribed upon the human consciousness.

The sabbath was and is such an opportunity and we too must jealously guard our day of rest. What is at stake here is not the mere observance of a holy day but the perpetuation of the deepest knowledge of God. Men are not born with well developed knowledge of God. They are born only with a deep longing and hunger for God, a need for God which will be filled one way or another. They can learn about what God has done and what he promises to do only by being told. The knowledge of God must be handed down from one generation to another, it must be taught and learned. When people don't know much about chemistry or mathematics they cannot possibly be scientists. When people know little about their own language, they find it difficult if not impossible to communicate effectively. And when people are religious illiterates, they cannot have a sense of the reality and the greatness of God. Because they have not learned their lessons, they keep asking the same questions over and over again in every generation. They cannot build upon the faith of those who have gone before them; their knowledge of God is stalled and stilted; it remains in a state of perpetual adolescence in a world which demands spiritual maturity.

In spite of our pride at being so well educated as to understand ourselves and the world in which we live, we have only to read the Bible to see how little we know of God and his works and ways, and how much we still have to learn about the profound and basic facts of life and death. These are truths which once were common knowledge, passed down by patient telling and retelling. If people are contented in their religious ignorance, perhaps it is because they are no longer sure that God is particularly important. They have a vague notion that it would be a good thing for their children to know something about the Bible, and their teenagers something about the catechism. If the weather is neither too bad to keep them home nor so good as to lure them to the shore, they will get their youngsters to Sunday school and themselves to church, though if anyone should ask them why, they would perhaps find it difficult to say.

These are the people who take great care not to let God get out of hand. He is the sort of jealous person who will not be content with a few hours on Sunday morning, and the first thing they know, he will be wanting to take over their whole life! To guard against this possibility it becomes necessary to restrict him to one day of the week, and here is where this command-ment is so convenient. Ask most people how to keep this commandment and they will say, "Go to church every Sunday." Any occasion for worship which falls on a weekday is easily shrugged off. Thus we see the twen-tieth-century phenomenon of Thanksgiving football and Thanksgiving parades and Thanksgiving dinners, in short, a day of Thanksgiving devoted to everything except to giving thanks. The reason we have come to take these weekday holidays so lightly is precisely because they are weekdays. Once we have done our duty by going to church on Sunday, we are sure that neither God nor the church has any right to expect any more of us. If we were quite honest, we would probably have to admit that one of the reasons we feel so good on Sunday noon is because we have fulfilled our religious obligation for that week; we are in the clear until the next Sunday rolls around again. Having done what God wanted us to do, we can relax and do what we want to do.

We are grateful for this commandment not because it gives us an opportunity to meet God but because it gives us a day off from work. How nice it is that we can do most anything we care to do on Sunday—in sharp contrast to the puritanical ways of our forefathers. We imagine this to be a kind of freedom, but actually we are no closer to the true meaning of Sunday than was the strict Sabbatarianism of bygone days. No longer content with one day off a week, it must be two days off, and soon it may well be three days off. What this means is that most people don't care much for their work. The most meaningful hours of their lives are their weekends, not their weekdays. They live all week long for Friday night, and are ardent members of the "Thank-Goodness-It's-Friday Club." This is the tragedy of life from which God has been driven. It becomes dull and meaningless, a thing to be escaped from. Work is unsatisfying and to be pursued for as short a time as possible. Leisure too has become a kind of monster which must be filled with all sorts of diversions in order to pass the time. If we are relieved when it is Friday, we are also a little glad for Monday morning and the regular routine which will deliver us from the exacting business of trying to keep ourselves entertained. And so we wish our lives away, waiting for Friday and then waiting for Monday morning again. What can this mean but that our lives are empty and devoid of meaning? It is into such lives, swept and clean, that the devil comes with seven friends more terrible than himself. Time becomes an enemy, and anything which will stop or slow it down becomes our friend. Sex, alcohol, and drugs are popular chiefly because they help people escape momentarily from time.

There was a time when people believed that every day belonged to God, that work was God's gift to us, and that like every gift it is holy. "To labor is to pray," the monks used to say in the Middle Ages. It was St. Jerome who said, "All the work of believers is prayer." And Martin Luther loved to quote an old proverb, "He who works faithfully prays twice." If such statements are used to make people accept disagreeable working conditons or the boredom which comes from an impersonal economic system, then they are not true. But if they are the honest confession of a Christian worker, then they come close to the heart of the third command. Having spent ourselves in honest toil in the service of God and man, we come to the close of the week properly prepared for the rest which God gives. Be sure of it, the sabbath comes from God. If men had their way there would be no such thing as a sabbath rest devoted to *God*. Year by year we can observe the steady whittling away of this time. The sound of church bells can barely be heard above the power mowers. What has happened is not so much that men have violated a holy day, as that they have lost the reality of a holy God. And without God, nothing is holy. Without God, time is a drag, work is a bore, and leisure is self-destructive.

This is a dead-end, and the only way out of a dead-end is to turn around. And when we do, there is God, waiting to crowd in on us, waiting to fill us and to free us. He is never far from us. But we cannot spend our time in contemplation. We have our work to do, work which will demand our attention and our energy, work which God has given and which he blesses. We cannot always be thinking of God or even be consciously aware of him. But let there be a lull, and God comes rushing in to fill the void. Let there be a break, and the earnest seeker after God will seize it as an opportunity for reaching out to him. It is no accident that God has arranged for a day of rest and worship.

Remember the sabbath. As if we could forget! Without it we would starve to death. How poor we make ourselves if we imagine that worship is an obligation, or the church a burden. This is where God becomes a reality. This is where he speaks his word to us. This is where we come alive. For this command too becomes a promise. In the structured routine of our life in time, God wants and waits to meet us.

5

Love Begins at Home

"Honor your father and your mother, that your days may be long in the land which the Lord your God gives you."

—*Exodus 20:12*

The Ten Commandments are not a haphazard collection of "dos and don'ts." They are an organic unity in which one command grows out of and rests upon the one which preceeds it. The whole of the Decalogue evolves from the opening affirmation, "I am the Lord your God." From this it follows that there can be no other gods, that God is to be addressed in trust and with respect, and that he is to be given a place in the ordered structure of time and history. Given such faith, prayer, and worship, God will be provided with the doorways through which he can enter into human lives and human history and by his presence transform them. That God will be satisfied with nothing less than such a transformation of humanity and history is indicated by the second table of the law in which is delineated man's obligation to his fellowmen. On close examination, these commandments also may be seen to be critical points of contact through which God enters into human relationships to redeem and reshape them.

The inevitable human tendency is to imagine that love for God can be divorced from love for man. We have known persons who were or who appeared to be deeply religious but who had little if any regard for their fellowmen. More than a few men of inspired words have left behind uninspired biographies, dramatizing the dichotomy within which we are tempted to live out our life with God. We have also known people who seemed to have no religion at all, who yet were kind, honest, and generous in their dealings with others, loving to their families, loyal to their friends, and helpful to strangers. Putting two such people together, one who has religion without love and another who has love without religion, it would be easy to conclude that religion and love are unrelated. This is just the reason some perceptive people in our day have turned away from religion as offering little creative help for the improvement of human relations.

But whatever religion it is such people are reacting against, it is not authentic Christian faith. The Bible everywhere speaks of these two loves, love for God and love for man, as a single love, like an equation which must have two equal sides if it is to balance. Change either side by even the smallest part and the whole equation falls apart. Love for God and love for man cannot be successfully separated for very long. Where love for God does not result in love for man, religion becomes bland and introspective, deprived of all its joy and adventure, faith is reduced to a vague feeling of religiosity, and the power of God is replaced by a puny,

tedious organization. And love for man which is not
rooted and grounded in love for God ultimately becomes
one-dimensional, a concern which is sincere, but without
depth of insight or courage of purpose.

The first point at which our life with God is brought
to bear upon our life with men is in our family relationships. Within the home the pattern for all subsequent
relationships is established. It is no good trying to be
loving to people far removed from us without first giving attention to those within our own household. If
these most personal of all human ties take on divine
dimensions, we will have provided for ourselves a home
base from which to operate, a center of strength, an oasis
of stability in a changing, unpredictable world, and a
pattern of love which will permeate our whole life.

When we listen to this commandment as it must have
sounded to the nomadic Israelites who first recorded it,
we hear overtones of God's promise to Abraham concerning a land which his descendents would possess and
inhabit. Abraham had himself been led to that land.
He had raised a son there, and his son Isaac had raised
two sons there. Jacob, the grandson of Abraham, had
no less than twelve sons in a dramatic fulfillment of
God's prediction of many descendents. But all this had
been many generations before. It was a dim memory
kept alive among the miserable slaves in Egypt. When
their life became unbearable they would remind each
other of their splendid origins and of the glorious future
which God had promised to Abraham. Now they were
on their way back to their land to take God up on his

promise. They had suffered long enough. Now they were entitled to be free and prosperous. If God meant what he said to Abraham they were certainly going to be there for their share. And so this commandment comes as a kind of warning to them. The land which was lost once could be lost again. It had been lost when ten brothers turned on one brother to sell him as a slave; the descendents of those brothers had themselves become slaves. They lost their land when they lost their honor. And they lost their honor because they forgot who they were. Their ability to survive as a nation would depend on the way in which they honored their parents, for such honor is possible only when people have recognized and accepted their own identity.

To this very day the Jewish people remain remarkable and admirable for their uncanny ability to survive the most incredible hardships and persecutions ever endured by any race of people and for the close-knit loyalty of their family life. These two qualities are, of course, directly related. Judge Drenk, the much honored head of the juvenile court of Burlington County, New Jersey, reports that in all the years of his distinguished career as a jurist a Jewish boy or girl has never appeared before him; and this not because Jewish children never get into trouble, but because their difficulties are usually handled within the family before they become involved with the law. A young Jewish lad caught breaking into a church was brought into the parsonage by his father and there in the pastor's presence was given a lecture on the honor of his father's name which that boy will not forget to his dying day. Out in the car sat his sister, his mother and his grandmother, all crying. Their boy was in trouble and so they were all in trouble with him. No doubt this lad will one day be successful, and his family will share his pride in achievement as they took part in his difficulties. Such family solidarity cannot fail to be a source of great strength to a person, and the lack of such solidarity is often a first point of weakness and failure.

This is the point at which this command to the ancient nomadic Israelites becomes universally valid for human existence. No one can understand and accept himself for what he is until he has resolved the tension between his need for and his independence of his parents. From the human point of view, fatherhood and motherhood are almost completely accidental. They depend on factors of biology and emotion over which we have slight control. Life takes on significance and meaning only when it is seen as part of something larger than mere procreation and becomes part of the creative activity of God. When men have searched for words by which they might speak of God they have found none more full of meaning than Father. We do not call God Father because he is like other fathers we have ever known; rather, we call ourselves fathers because at an important point in our children's lives we stand in the place of God to them. This is not because we might somehow hope to replace God, but because we occupy the position and fulfill the need which will one day be held by God. We do not say of parents that they look like their children. We say of children that they resemble their parents. When we speak of God's image in man we do not mean to suggest that God looks like us, but that in some way we are like God, that when he looks at us he sees, or hopes to see, something of himself in us. And when our children look at us (and what could be more humbling or demanding than this?), they look to see something of God in us; they honor not so much their parents as their parents' God. God has so arranged our human affairs that at a certain point he depends on us to represent him in the tiny lives which are being formed within our homes and families. It is no accident that we speak of "our father's God," since for most of our lifetime our relation to God and our relation to our parents are so closely bound together that we can hardly think of one without thinking also of the other.

We are also called the sons of God. When Jesus walked this earth in human flesh he called God his Father, and we have learned to call him the Son: Son of God and Son of man. If to be a parent is to be something like God, to be a child is to be something like the eternal Son. There is within the life of Christ a balanced tension between independence and obedience which made it possible for him to be both utterly himself and yet completely responsive to his heavenly Father. Independence from and obedience to our parents present us with a similar tension, one which we are not usually successful in balancing, becoming either so independent of our parents that we lose touch with them, or so dependent on them that we cannot make our own way in the world. In any case we never stop being children. But just as the child learns to replace an earthly parent with a heavenly one, so we must learn to move out from an earthly childhood to becoming sons of God. What this will mean, in terms of this commandment, is that we can accept our parents for what they are and forgive them for what they are not. It also means that we can step back and watch our children surpass us, knowing that they are beckoned and challenged by another greater parent than we could ever hope to be.

The Ten Commandments have already asserted the creative power of God, and now they indicate that we are ourselves a part of that creativity. We fashion our children's faith and personalities by what we are. Our children's physical bodies will be determined by our genes, but their souls are shaped by our faith. We have a responsibility not only to our own children but to all children. The determinative influence in a child's life may not be his father or mother at all. If the child is adopted, the adopting parents will have far more to do with shaping what that child is to become than will the real parents. For some children an older brother or sister, an aunt or an uncle, a teacher or a pastor will be the focal and crucial point in determining the future. This puts all of us on constant guard. Whether we choose it to be so or not, we cannot escape the fact that we leave our mark, for better or for worse, upon the generation which comes after us.

But the impressive and interesting thing about this commandment is that it puts the burden of responsibility not on the parents, where we might expect it to be laid, but on the children. It is not the parents who are commanded to love their children, but the children who are instructed to honor their parents. Nor does the commandment mention loving one's parents. It says only that we are to honor them. Love, of course, cannot be commanded. Love must grow spontaneously or not at all. What can be commanded are the conditions within which such love is possible.

Few children are in a position to be able to love their parents maturely. Mostly, when we are growing up we are more conscious of our parents' shortcomings than we are of their lovable qualities. At best they seem limited, and at worst they seem cruel. Only when we get far enough away from them to be able to see them against the background of other people can we appreciate them for what they are. Mark Twain observed that a boy of seventeen is sure his father knows nothing, and at twenty-one is amazed to discover how much his father has learned in four years. The commandment does not require us to imagine that our parents are the greatest people in the world. To a child, of course, his mother is beautiful, just as to a mother her baby is beautiful. Most of us can and do thank God for our parents. But some people have reason to regret their parents. This does not mean they cannot honor them. It means that all of us, no matter how good or bad our parents are or were, may honor them not only for what they are, but for what they might have been, for what they were intended to be. This way we can forgive them for what they were not, and we do not have to make our children suffer for what we may have missed.

One result of the popularity of psychology is the tendency to *blame* our parents for what we are. It is true, of course, that a person's personality will be shaped to a large degree by his relation to his parents. But while this may explain what we are, it does not excuse what we are. There comes a time when we can and must detach ourselves and become mature, responsible adults. This happens when we honor our parents for what they were and forgive them for what they were not, remembering that they also were once children with parents, that they too had their burdens to carry with them, and perhaps did better by us than we had any right to expect if we could have known all that they knew. Parents are, after all, only symbols for a deeper, more lasting parenthood. Behind the limited human beings we call father and mother there is a divine parent with the strength of all fathers and the love of all mothers. All of us, parents and children alike, must learn to lean on this deeper strength and love of God. Only then can we come to understand who we really are: the children of God, created in his image. Only then do we have a reason for taking up space in a crowded world.

How strange it sounds to modern ears to hear that land is given to men by God. We are so sure that the little piece of ground we call (or one day hope to call) our own is ours because we hold a clear title to it. But who is to say to whom any part of this earth ultimately belongs? No matter how far back we may be able to trace the claims on any given property, there is probably someone else before that who could contest our right of ownership. Most of our land was taken by force from the Indians. No doubt they in their turn had to fight with some other ancient tribe for possession of it. At best our hold upon the land is tentative and our future on it is dependent far more upon our ability to survive as worthy human beings than on our prosperity or our stubbornness or our strong defenses. The record of history is pretty clear at this point. Whenever men have valued land more than the people who lived on it, they have lost their land and their people. But where they prize the dignity and worth of a single human being beyond the price of any real estate, there and only there is to be found a civilization which has the promise of survival. And the place where such worth is established is in the home. For where children are seen as a gift from God and where parents are honored and respected as if they spoke in his place, there life takes on importance and value which it can get in no other place. And if one's own children are a gift, then all children are a gift to someone. If one's own parents are honored, then all elders are to be respected and looked up to. The health of any nation may be measured by the way in which the elder citizen is regarded. Where old age becomes a burden to be dreaded, there people are in trouble. But where the aged are honored, cared for, and listened to with respect for the accumulated wisdom of their years, there is hope for the future.

The cult of youth which is so popular just now is the

symptom of a serious displacement of values. We cannot expect our young people to act with great respect toward their elders so long as they are surrounded by adults who are not especially concerned about the welfare of the old. Now and again one hears the comment, "When I was young I never got away with being as fresh as kids are nowadays." For all its apparent moral concern, such a remark conceals a great deal of hostility. It betrays smoldering resentment for long past repressions, and jealousy of youthful freedom. Thus, ironically, we may observe young people trying to grow up too fast and adults attempting to stay youthful too long. What has happened is that age is no longer honored, and so the structure for healthy relationships between the generations has come apart at the seams, with young people resenting adults and adults resenting and exploiting the teen-ager. What is called for here is awakened recognition of the honor of age. The problems of the aging cannot and must not be shaken off as none of our concern. Our survival as a nation may well be more dependent on our concerted action in providing medical care for the aged than upon the strength of our defenses. We are not entitled to assume any automatic guarantee of survival by honoring our parents, as if God were making some sort of deal with us. But it is still true that if we will learn to honor the past generation, we may begin to understand the present, and so have hope for the future.

6

Life Without Price

"You shall not kill."

—*Exodus 20:13*

All the commandments are important, since none could be eliminated without damage to the architecture of love which together they construct. Yet it may sometimes happen that one of the ten will emerge to speak with special relevance to a given need in a particular age. The command for our generation would seem to be the commandment about killing.

Ours is an enlightened age. From all outward appearances, life has never seemed to hold as many possibilities as it does just now. Diseases which have baffled and plagued mankind for centuries have been all but eliminated. Automation and labor-saving devices promise relief from the drudgery of meaningless work. A general rise in living standards has put comparative wealth within reach of more people than ever before in recorded history. All this ought to mean that life has at last been given the central place it deserves in the total scheme of things, that the value of life has become the standard by which all other wealth is measured. But

even a casual glance at the contemporary scene is
enough to demonstrate that this is far from true. There
is instead an alarming amount of evidence, from the
slums in our cities to the traffic on our highways, that
life is still cheap, that humanity is still expendable.

This low estimate of the value of life is frightening
not because it is new but because the possibilities for
killing are so much greater than the ancient Israelites
ever dreamed. Life in Old Testament times was crude
and primitive. Killing was a common and constant occur-
rence. The Israelites do not appear to have been much
better than their contemporaries in this regard. They
eliminated human sacrifice from their religion, which
represents progress of a kind, but they got themselves
involved in some pretty bloody slaughter in the con-
quering of the land called holy, bloodshed which they
cheerfully claimed was directed by the Creator of all
life. One of the perplexing moral difficulties we have
with the Old Testament is the great amount of killing
it contains, only some of which seems to have been even
militarily necessary. How does it happen that the same
people who gave to the world this commandment should
also have seen it as the will of God that they should do
away with the population of whole cities?

Here we must note that this commandment does not
say, as we commonly imagine, "You shall not kill other
human beings." It says, "You shall not kill," period. All
life is created by God. All life is a sacred, holy mystery.
Killing of any kind is at best a cruel necessity, and at
worst a kind of dis-creation which sets man in direct

opposition to the giver of life. Albert Schweitzer is our time's best known pleader for an attitude of reverence for life. A doctor who has held in his hand a scalpel, knowing that just one faulty stroke could mean the difference between life and death, understands that life is the profoundest mystery of all. The man of medicine has traditionally been accorded an honor only slightly less than that given to the religious leader, and in some primitive cultures the practice of religion and of medicine merge into one. Life is that elusive quality given each of us to enjoy for awhile before it slips irretrievably away. Life is all we know—this time between our birth and death when we must succeed or fail, when we make our contribution or commit our crimes. Everything we desire and everything God commands depends on life. Without it neither man's potentialities nor God's expectations have any meaning.

Self-preservation is common to all forms of life. No living thing willingly or gladly parts with life. And yet killing is a part of life. Life is sustained by devouring other life. Birds live on insects. Cats kill mice. The wild animals of the jungle and forest stalk and kill each other. And human beings depend for their food on the beasts of the field and on the fruits of the earth. We cannot live without killing. How then can God command us not to kill? *The same with plant life.*

At this point we touch close to the heart of the Old and New Testaments. From the opening pages of the Bible worship is related to sacrifice. The first born from the flock or the first fruits of the field were to be given to God before man killed that which he would need for his own sustenance. Such a sacrifice served as a reminder that life is a holy gift, and that if killing is a part of the cruel reality within which man must live in an imperfect world, his own share in that blood-letting must be minimal and reluctant. What horrifies us is not that men should sometimes kill, but that they should enjoy killing. By inserting an innocent death in the constant round of deaths, man is made to remember that no living thing was made to die, that all death is tragic.

But if death is tragic, it also is inevitable. Since all things must one day die, it would be possible to argue that killing cannot be so bad, since it is only a hastening of that which would have happened sooner or later anyway. But there is a profound difference between senseless death and meaningful death. Meaningful death is an avenue to meaningful life and a redemption of death itself. Here we confront the holy mystery of the cross, the death of Christ, where God put his own price tag on life by exchanging his life for ours. Christ died because all men violate this commandment. We killed the Son of God. And yet that death became the means by which God offers life to his executioners. The innocent one turns on his accusers and forgives them. The tragedy of death becomes the victory of God and the hope of men. One has died for many.

Man slays in order that he himself might live. The Son of God dies so that all others might live. If death cannot be avoided, it can be redeemed and filled with meaning. Only when men have learned how to face death can they learn how to live. Life that is lived for itself is doomed. The only life which has hope is that life which enables others to live. This is the living sacrifice of which Paul writes in Romans. Mankind has come the full round. His life with God began in human sacrifice— a pagan, bloody rite by which the weakest and most innocent were put to death in order to assure the survival of those least deserving of life. Now man in Christ is enabled to "forget himself into greatness," in the phrase of Emerson, to lay down his life in loving service so that others might live.

So how do we stand at mid-twentieth century as regards the fifth commandment and its affirmation concerning the infinite value of human life? Outright murder is rather rare among us. It is still infrequent enough to warrant front page headlines. But there are other kinds of murder, some of them so subtle as almost to escape detection and here our record is not so good. This, after all, is the atomic age, the age of over-kill and of radioactive fallout. Since the days of the first atomic bomb, a new moral principle has been introduced into human affairs. The first atomic bomb was excused on the ground that it killed fewer people than would have died in a full-scale invasion of Japan. It is supposed to have brought the war to a speedy end. Now we are hearing the same argument in relation to nuclear testing. We are told that there is a hazard to such tests, but that the risk is so small that the tests will cause only one or two babies out of so many hundreds of thousands to die or be born malformed. So some have argued in test-ban treaty debates that we are justified in risking the possible death of a few babies in order to provide ourselves with a destructive power as great as any potential enemy.

To see the flaw in this argument it is necessary to ask only one question: whose baby ought to die so that the rest of us can go on living? As Abraham stood with his knife poised over the heart of his son, he was ready to make such a sacrifice, and I will try to honor him for it. But I am not so ready. I will not risk my children's lives for my own, and I will not ask anyone else to risk theirs. Nothing is changed by the fact that we can never know which of all the children who die are dying because of the fall-out, and that our guilt is therefore faceless and anonymous. The fact remains that we have no right to poison the earth's atmosphere. What our enemy does our enemy will have to account for. Our morals cannot and must not be adjusted in order to accommodate our enemy.

The time has come when we must send representatives prepared for serious disarmament negotiation rather than for cynical propaganda bouts in which neither side is really ready to give up anything. To an alarming extent, our national economy is being tied to our national defense, so that the time may come when we can no longer afford to disarm. General Eisenhower made this his parting warning when he left public office. Nations which depend on huge military establishments to maintain their economy cannot afford to be peace loving. They need always to search for enemies in order to justify their defense expenditures. They will trade their friends and enemies around almost at will so as to be certain always of having someone to hate badly enough to justify the need for strong defenses. America has not yet reached such a point, but we need to watch carefully.

There is another form of murder going on all around us which we seldom describe as murder, but which belongs in any serious twentieth-century discussion of this commandment. There are two ways of killing people. One is by fatally wounding their bodies. The other is by breaking their spirits so that they no longer have the will to live with the dignity and the potential greatness God gave them. Of the two, I am not sure but that the second is not worse than the first. Perhaps this has already happened to the American Indian. It came very close to happening to the American Negro. There is nothing sadder than the sight of a human being who, though intended by God to live like a man, cowers and kowtows as though he were an inferior creature. What a tribute to the strength of the human spirit that these people, after so many generations of degradation, still are not broken and resigned. One of the noblest struggles going on anywhere in the world is the non-violent struggle for equal rights which is taking place among us.

No one believes that such a struggle ought to be necessary in a democracy. Persons in their right minds no longer think that people are either superior or inferior because of the color of their skin. But lip service to brotherhood is not changing this tragic situation quickly enough to prevent it from exploding in our face. We like to say that racial discrimination will take care of itself if given time. But time is the one thing we do not have. The minority races will no longer be satisfied with being told that perhaps their grandchildren may one day enjoy the privileges we have now. They want those privileges now too, and they will get them one way or another.

The one instance in which Christians have sometimes felt justified in taking the life of another is in the capital punishment of a convicted murderer. They are even able to point out biblical support for such a custom. Unfortunately, once this scriptural injunction concerning the punishment of murder is taken at face value, there is no reason for not also following the Old Testament punishment for adultery and idolatry. Here is where the case for capital punishment falls apart. Once any part of the Mosaic law is naively transferred to the twentieth century, then the whole body of that law becomes valid. Not even the most ardent proponent of capital punishment would care to also demand the death penalty for, say, homosexuality, as does the law of Moses. By what ground then does he pick and choose among these laws, claiming validity for some and not for others?

There is not the slightest evidence that fear of execution has ever deterred anyone from a crime of violence. It is even possible that one violence begets another. The very words "capital punishment" are a contradiction in terms. Punishment which results in someone's death is not punishment at all. It is revenge. Punishment assumes correctability. But to punish by death is to take away the very possibility of correction. Who is helped by capital punishment? The murdered one cannot be brought back by it. The murderer is not helped, nor is "society," that amorphous entity which is supposed to demand restitution for murder. Even if there were no possibility that a wrong verdict might be handed down, capital punishment would still encourage self-destructive indignation and revenge. Clearly it would be better that ten guilty persons should go free than that one should be innocently executed.

Murderers are not created overnight. They have often had many years of training in hatred and violence. They have had so much help along the way—too many people have let them down—that it is necessary to say that all of society is involved in every act of violence. If we fear that such persons may not pay for their crime, let it be remembered that guilt is often borne in a thousand different ways. And there is hope for all men. God is the God of hopeless cases. Even the lowliest of sinners is entitled to time for the amendment of his life.

"You shall not kill," God says. But you shall make alive. You will be ready to lay down your own lives and thus you will succeed in bringing life to others. The healing touch of your medical skill will bring new hope and life to thousands who would otherwise have died. Your moral courage will make it possible for you to forgive and understand your enemy without selling out to him. This courage will enable men realistically to grasp both corporate and individual evil and guilt, and it will enable men to deal creatively with the real causes for disagreement between persons and nations.

The possibilities for brotherhood which are given to us will make it possible to end the incredible waste of human resources which results from racial prejudice, and to enable each man to rise as high as he can, as high as he will. Something happens to us all when any of our brothers reaches for a star.

The experience of Christians in every age has been that God meets them and speaks to them in their neighbor's need. Where any man responds in love to another's need, there God is at work. For it is God who alone can make us sensitive to the true necessities of someone whose chief claim on us is that we may be able to help. It is God who makes it possible for us to rise above self interest and go to their rescue at whatever sacrifice to ourselves. And it is God who prevents us from being so proud of justice and love that we imagine ourselves to have helped, and so play at being god.

Sacrificial love is under some suspicion just now. Ayn Rand argues that it is the real cause of disagreements among men, that only enlightened self-interest can save us. Such a philosophy is tempting if only because self-interest is less strenuous and more manageable than selfless love. But the historic record of enlightened self-interest is not reassuring. This is the way to anarchy, since it sets up impassable gulfs between men and nations. Christian love presupposes that each man has stood where his neighbor stands and has seen the world through his eyes. He has acted as though he received when he gave, not that he might derive satisfaction from his giving but rather that he might understand what and when and how to give. He spends the coinage of his life in reckless abandon, and leaves behind a world made better for his having been a part of it.

7

Love is a Four-Letter Word

"You shall not commit adultery."

—*Exodus* 20:14

Words, like people, have personalities. They are born, they mature, they become worn out, and are cast aside to be replaced by newer, fresher words. But some words are so basic they are irreplaceable, and when these foundation words become distorted by misuse, losing their meaning and vitality, then we are all in trouble. Priceless words like "freedom," "democracy," and "peace" have become victims of the cold war, meaning all things to all people, depending on who is using them and how he wants them to be understood.

Another word which is in trouble now is "love." This ought to be one of the grandest, most beautiful words in our language. How could we say "I love you" if we had no word for love, and how could we live if we could not speak our love? And yet this word has come to mean so many things to so many people that it is in danger of being hopelessly misshapen. Alice in Wonderland once observed, "A word means what I want it to mean and nothing else." For some people, love is so noble and lofty an emotion that it would be sullied by any suggestion of animal attraction. For others, love is a cheap and ugly sensation, a physical reaction between two people who are otherwise strangers to one another. Both these views of love are distortions of the real thing, and of the two it would be difficult to say which has done the greater harm to a realistic, biblical understanding of love.

In the early centuries of the church, Christianity was plagued by people called Gnostics. The Gnostics used just enough biblical terminology to sound like good Christians, but their Christianity was confused by pagan ideas. One of their notions was that God created men's souls and the devil created men's bodies. This meant that spiritual things were good and physical things were evil. Therefore the way to be good was to deny the body and encourage the soul. This sounds just enough like some things Paul had said, that even after the Gnostics were declared heretics some of their ideas crept into the church anyway. One result of this was the notion that the way to be really holy was to stay single. Paul too had recommended the single life, but on the quite different grounds that the shortness of time remaining to the church had created an emergency situation for Christians. Nonetheless, the authority of Paul was used to justify a separation of humanity into the religious, who were celibate, and the rest of the people, who were married. The religious were supposed to be holier and purer because they were celibate. This seemed to suggest that physical relations between men and women are somewhat evil. To this day, the Roman church insists that Mary was a virgin not only before Christ was born, but even after his birth, as if it would detract from her holiness if she had had other children in the usual way by her husband Joseph.

Protestants too have played their part in this tradition. Sex has often been thought of as unmentionable. God-fearing Christians have been expected to act as though sex did not exist, or that it were the invention of the devil. Western civilization has inherited a guilty conscience about sex. Needless to say, the teaching that sex inevitably involves sin and guilt causes far more problems than it solves—and is far from any realistic assessment of human life. Persons tend to come in one of two genders, so the subject of sex is pretty difficult to avoid indefinitely.

Lately there has been a libertarian reaction which has taken up the opposite extreme. According to this new mythology, repression is supposed to be very unhealthy. The only thing to do is to throw off all inhibitions. Virginity is supposed to be prudish and unnecessary. Sex is seen as just another animal function with no more significance than eating dinner or taking a walk. This kind of uninhibited life is a lot easier to talk and write about than it is to practice, but the libertine tends to blame the squares around him for the difficulty he finds in implementing his philosophy, as if, left to himself, he might be able to work things out to his own satisfaction. He seldom recognizes the anti-social orientation of his rebellion. By an interesting meeting of extremes, the inhibited puritan and the uninhibited libertine arrive at exactly the same conclusion, that sex and love are unrelated.

Against both these extremes must be set the realistic view of the Bible, in which the human body is the creation of God and like all of his creation is both good and beautiful. The Bible insists that sex and love belong together, and that what God has brought together, man must not put asunder.

The commandment, "Thou shalt not commit adultery," is God's defense of love. He has everything at stake in the saving of this word. He is love and if men are incapable of responding to love, then they are unable to respond to God. So it is essential that he meet us at the point of our most intimate relationships and help us to turn our love away from ourselves.

God is always immensely practical. He understands that love is nothing until it has been given concrete, visible, physical expression. Until this happens, what we take to be love is most often self-love, our love for a projected image rather than for another human being of flesh and blood. So long as we are loving only fantasies and phantoms, we cannot be related at the deepest level to another human being. God has seen that it is not good for man to be alone, and so he gives us a mate. This is one of God's ways of enabling us to escape the vast well of loneliness in which the loveless live, and to relate ourselves to someone else at the deepest, truest level of our existence. Here is one of the points which determines whether we are to hide in the shell of our own self-pity or to grow through someone else into a person larger than we could have been all by ourselves.

Love is a relationship between two people by which both of them together are better, stronger people than either of them could be alone. True love means that two people have become indispensable to one another, that they have become a part of one another, so that when one is gone the other is not quite complete. This is true of marriage, of a deep and lasting friendship, and of our life with God. This commandment is God's way of protecting those fine and intimate relationships of life by which we grow and are made strong. The legal meaning of adultery can be applied only to married people, but the sixth commandment has something important to say to everyone. It is saying in effect that we must learn to love other people for what they are, not for how they make us feel. Love which is adulterated is love which has been "made inferior or impure by the mixture of a poorer substance leaving the visible result with the appearance of being genuine." Adulterated love is love so cluttered up with illusions and fantasies that what is loved is an image, not a genuine human being.

This is an experience which all married persons have had. They fall in love, or imagine that they do, and find themselves thinking about their beloved, and mentally creating an image with all sorts of wonderful qualities. By the time they are married they are certain that their partner is the most beautiful and the most ideal person in the world. Then one day after the honeymoon is over they wake up to discover that they have not married a vision; they have married a flesh and blood human being whom they don't know very well. All this time they have been loving an image, a mental construct. And this person whom they have married does not correspond to the image at all. At this point, it would be very easy for them to conclude that their marriage is a failure, but what has happened is that these two people now are learning to love each other for what they really are. They are learning, perhaps for the first time in their lives, to love another human being who possesses weakness and strength, beauty and unseemliness. If they are ever to become one flesh, as it says in the wedding service, they must break down all the walls of misunderstanding, fear, and guilt. Only when these walls are gone can their relations say, "I love you." So long as these barriers exist, to that extent their relations must say, "I love me," perhaps even, "I hate you." Many a married person who has never considered infidelity has nevertheless offered to his partner such adulterated love.

The tragedy of adultery is that it produces a person incapable of loving anyone other than himself. It is no accident that where morals are the loosest the divorce rate is the highest. There is no longer a capability for the kind of love necessary for a successful and satisfying marriage. Adulterers imagine themselves to be emancipated when in fact they have closed the doors of love on themselves and are shut tightly inside. The uninhibited talk a good line but their performance is not impressive. The fact of the matter is that love must be carefully built over many years; it does not happen easily and without effort. It is the result of joys and sorrows shared, of victories won and defeats suffered together until a genuine partnership has been established. But such love is so wonderful a thing that it is worth all it costs. Once a person has known such love, he would not dream of trading it for a fleeting moment of selfish passion.

This commandment also has something important to say to people before their marriage. Now and again adults will take the hard line against teenagers going steady. Their intention is sound even if their means are doubtful, for one of the surest ways of encouraging anything among adolescents is by making it wickedly forbidden. Still, young people ought to be themselves, and not premature copies of adults. Nothing in this world will stop young people from falling in love with each other. This has been happening as long as there have been boys and girls, and it will go on happening until the end of time. And there is no reason why it should not. Young people are so attractive that we cannot help loving them, even when they irritate us and it is only natural that such lovely creatures should fall in love with one another. Who can forget the first girl he ever loved? Puppy love is one of the precious and fragile wonders of human existence. There is a radiant, innocent purity about such love which is joyous to behold. And promiscuity can only spoil such love, not because sex itself is sinful, but because it is always wrong to turn another human being into an object, a mere means for gratifying selfish desires. A person owes it to himself and to his future partner to be able to offer a pure and unadulterated love.

This is not easy, to be sure. We are surrounded by suggestive temptations which make this daily more difficult. The world has so reversed its values that it pays more attention to the infidelities of an underweight American actress and her English boy friend than it does to the serious concerns of civilization. One hardly knows whether to be more nauseated by the newspapers which print every sordid detail of these carefully staged affairs or by the public which devours them so eagerly. It is in this milieu that our teen-agers are learning their lessons only too well.

Such travesties only serve to underscore the rarity and beauty of genuine love, the love for which the sixth command is pleading. In its envy the world will always insist that such love is square, that it is dull and unexciting. This is a trick the world has always used. Evil knows how to wear a lovely face, like the movie sets which are all facade and have nothing behind them. Here is a temptation implicit in every human relationship: that people will be valued chiefly for what they can do for us. Friends are often chosen because they are the kind of people it is profitable to be associated with, and neighbors are valued because they are the kind of people it is fashionable to be seen with. We can be unfaithful to a friend, not through any intention, but just when we have nothing to gain by looking them up or calling them or dropping them a line. How poor we

make ourselves when we cut ourselves off from those
whom we have loved because we are unwilling to make
the effort to keep the lines of communication open.
This too is a kind of infidelity.

But real love is unfailingly fresh and exciting. It relates us to another human being at the deepest level,
and since nothing is more complicated and interesting
than a personality, we can spend a lifetime learning to
know one other person well. There will be something
different each day, so that love becomes a kind of
adventure.

When a human being has learned such openness and
honesty toward someone else, then all the doorways of
his personality are open, and God comes rushing in to
be so loved. It is no accident that God is more concerned
about our intimate life than is our closest friend or
partner. For when we must hide from those we love the
most, then we must also hide from God. And to hide
from God is to know him always as enemy and accuser
and as angry judge. "We love because God first loved
us," John says. At the center of our being, God intends
there to be the serenity of those who have been accepted
by their creator, who have known forgiveness, and who
can therefore accept themselves. Only so are we freed
from our eternal self-concern so as to be able to reach
out in love to someone else, to forgive and accept them
for what they are.

We cannot love without forgiveness, because the one
we love is never all that we hoped he would be, just
as we are never all that we hoped ourselves to be.

We cannot forgive until we have been forgiven. It is no accident that we pray, "Forgive us as we forgive." Our life with God and our life with those closest and dearest to us is all bound up together, so that God's love for us makes it possible for us to love, and our love for one other human being opens doorways in our personality by which God can build into us the length and breadth and height and depth of love. This is no romantic illusion, no noble and lofty fantasy uncontaminated by the smell of flesh. This is love in the most intimate and immediate sense. For God relates himself to us as bridegroom to his bride, which is to say, God gave himself for us and to us. The love he offers is nothing less than himself, that we might know and possess him in his fulness. So too, we may come to him, the walls and barriers of guilt removed, to give ourselves to him, that he might possess and fill us.

Our love for God is not ethereal, and neither is our love for one another. Love is a flesh and blood reaction given in time and space. Love is a four-letter word. It is spelled out in terms of our being or it is not love at all. Such love demands honesty and openness, and we should despair of ever knowing it were it not for this commandment, God's promise that the love we offer to one another can be the love which he, in his forgiving grace, intends. So may we love as we have been loved; with the utter faithfulness of God.

8

What's Mine is Yours

"You shall not steal."

—*Exodus 20:15*

A man is washed ashore on a deserted island. He is hungry. He walks about until he finds a fruit tree. But he does not know to whom the tree belongs, and so he decides not to eat because he does not want to take what does not belong to him. As night draws on he is cold. Walking further, he finds abandoned blankets which he could wrap about himself. But he does not know to whom the blankets belong, and so he walks on because he does not want to use something which is not his. He is tired. He longs to lie down and sleep. But he does not know to whom this land belongs, and he does not want to act as though it were his own. Is this an honorable man to be admired or a fool to be pitied?

Every day of our lives we take what does not belong to us. The air we breathe, the sunlight we absorb, the ideas we read, much that is essential to our lives comes without a legal transaction. We cannot live without taking that which is not our own and claiming it for ourselves. How foolish we would be if we were to refuse to breathe because we did not own the air. We need no other reason for taking it in than that we are alive. The world may not owe us a living, but it provides us with one all the same. It cannot very well deny us the space we occupy as we walk or sleep. There is a six foot plot for every human being who ever died. That space can never be taken away from us. We have neither to earn or deserve it. It is ours simply because we exist. Life is a gift. And so too is death.

In life we eat, and the fruit of the earth is absorbed into our flesh and becomes a part of us. In death we are absorbed back into the earth and become one with it once more. We cannot escape the elementary process of supply and demand. Since we are flesh and blood we cannot live without food, without clothing, without shelter of some kind. To deprive a person of these things is to deprive him of his life. To give these is to give life. The world is the great giver. This wonderful earth is capable of providing quite enough food for every human being on it. How does it happen then that there are starving people in the midst of such abundance?

We speak glibly about the affluent society we have created. But reality is not so kind. The sober truth is that even in prosperous America there are people who live their whole lives in hopeless hunger. And in less prosperous countries there is unbelievable poverty. Such deprivation is a grim reality for millions of people whose only crime is that they were born. They have no bright future, no hope. The gap between them and us grows with each advance we make. We are part of a world so structured as to permit these pockets of poverty. The world has enough food for everyone, yet some people starve while others throw food away. Who are the thieves in such a world?

This commandment plunges us squarely into a major conflict of the twentieth century. On the one side are the capitalists who say that man must earn his daily bread himself, and on the other are the communists who say that the state must provide it for him. This is not, to be sure, the whole story of the struggle between communism and capitalism. The cold war is not only a struggle between two competing economic systems, it is also an ideological struggle between two mutually contradictory views of man's nature and the meaning of human existence, and of course a political struggle between two great power blocs of nations. But since at their roots both capitalism and communism are economic systems, both are concerned about providing man with the physical necessities of life, and so both come under the judgment of this commandment.

The Bible does not endorse any particular system of economics, but it indicates that man's life with God and God's with man is intimately involved with daily bread. Two families sit down to eat. One eats with gratitude, the other does not. There will be no difference in how well they eat. But there will be a vast difference in *what* they eat. One will eat a merciful gift of God. The other, a loaf of bread. One family receives the fruits of the earth. The other takes them. And God has said we shall not steal. If God does not want us to take our bread, he must want us to receive it from him or from someone else. The seventh command relates God to our bread and to our neighbor's bread.

The first Christians recognized this instinctively and made a fumbling attempt to translate it into an economy. "Now the company of those who believed were of one heart and soul, and no one said that any of the things which he possessed was his own, but they had everything in common . . . there was not a needy person among them, for as many as were possessors of lands or houses sold them, and brought the proceeds of what was sold and laid it at the apostles' feet; and distribution we made to each as any had need" (Acts 4:32, 34-35). These early Christians did not claim divine inspiration for their little experiment, nor were they able to keep it going for very long. This particular New Testament experiment in economics broke down when some people withheld a few of their belongings, turning over only a part of what they owned to the common pool.

The Bible stands as a witness to the fact that the instinct to acquire and possess visible objects runs very strong among human beings. This attachment to things seems to be peculiarly human. Other animals prefer detachment and unencumbrance. But people hang on to material things in a way which has little to do with the value or usefulness of what is held. Where there is a fire, for example, people have a compulsion, amounting almost to an instinct, to rescue some object or other from the flames, almost as if they were thereby saving

a part of themselves. Perhaps this means that our possessions serve to reinforce our otherwise tenuous existence in an uncertain world. Material objects have
permanence; they can be weighed and measured and
controlled. They give us a sense of importance. Without
them we feel insecure and unnecessary.

This need for possession is the undoing of any variety
of communism. Communism would be effective only
where everyone was so perfectly unselfish as to work
always and only for the common good. The early Christians learned rather soon that entrance into the New
Testament church did not bring about immediate perfection. Communism in practice turns out never to be
as humanitarian as it appears in theory. Even the experiment in communism in the Book of the Acts had
to be severely enforced. Communism can survive anywhere only through strong controls and secret police.

Capitalism, on the other hand, not only assumes a
need for possession, it requires it. In practice capitalism
is seldom as heartless as it is pictured by its enemies,
but it does tend to isolate individuals from one another
by making them less dependent on other human beings
than on the system of which they are a part. An economic system must not be elevated above the humanity
it serves. Indebtedness is less immoral than hunger. Sol-
vency in the face of need cannot be justified. Systems
must be adapted and adjusted until they are able to do
what they are supposed to do, that is, to provide human
beings with the necessities of life. Americans have a
right to be prouder than they sometimes are of their

immense generosity, but this giving is extra-curricular.
Our system itself has somehow not responded to genuine human need as gracefully and as rapidly as we
might have expected, knowing the great good will of
most Americans. We must not be content, nor let our
leaders be content, until it does.

One of my earliest memories is of a wonderful book
of children's patterns, and among them was a book-plate
which read: "This book is the property of." Underneath,
a child could add his own name. I can remember making dozens of these plates and pasting them in every
book I could get my hands on. My father very soon
pointed out to me in graphic terminology, since most
of the books which bore this gallant legend were in
fact his own, that there is more to ownership than a
label. I can also remember serving as a secretary for a
Captain's Mast on board the ship on which I served in
the Navy. A sailor had stolen a jeep. His real crime was
that he had been so unwise as to steal it from the Army,
and relations between the Army and the Navy had taken
a turn for the worse just then. His argument, as I recall
it, was that if the Army didn't want its jeep to be stolen,
they should have posted a guard on it. So long as books
and jeeps are left lying about there will be always the
temptation to acquire them in the easiest way. The
books eventually came back to their owners bearing
souvenirs of my childish larceny; and the jeep was returned somewhat the worse for wear. By such experi-
ences I learned that there is more to possession than
acquisition. This, I think, is what this commandment is

trying to say. Existence reinforced by a kind of possession in which we have invested nothing of ourselves is essentially false and self-defeating.

This is the point at which gambling must be rejected as self-destructive. The incredible appeal of gambling lies in the possibility of acquiring the prestige of possession without being required to pay the price. Sometimes people talk as if it were the risk of gambling which makes it immoral. But all of life is a risk. Gambling would still be wrong even if it were a bet on a sure thing in which there was no risk at all. Presumably a person buys only that for which he has a need. What he hopes to gain from gambling is not the filling of a need but the acquiring of the prestige of possession for its own sake. The characteristic gambler is insecure. He needs the reassurance of possession. But this kind of acquisition never results in the satisfaction of genuine ownership, and so he feels more insecure than ever and must return to his gambling with even greater compulsion than before. Such compulsion is not present in every act of gambling, to be sure. But at the very least, all betting supports the structure of gambling from which the underworld of our society derives its major source of income. Every bet, no matter how innocent it may appear, even when, and perhaps especially when, it is made in church or on behalf of a charitable association, is in fact a subsidy of anti-social forces bent on destroying us all.

It would seem that people tend to take theft rather more seriously than almost any other crime. Yet shoplifting is becoming something of a national scandal. These two seemingly contradictory facts indicate that the values rated highest among us are material ones. Twice in my life I have been robbed. Once when I was a boy our home was broken into, and once since my marriage. This is a disturbing experience, as anyone who has gone through it can testify. It is not the loss which is upsetting. In neither case was anything of much value found to be missing. There are, after all, more fruitful fields for burglars than preachers' homes. I dare say that if someone had come to me and asked me for a handout in the amount which I lost I would have been soft-hearted enough to give it to him. But for someone to take the same amount away from me without my permission is something else again.

Now why should this be? Ten dollars gone is ten dollars gone, whether it is given away or stolen. The point, however, is that in a curious way our property is a part of ourselves. When we give a man ten dollars we are giving him more than a piece of currency. We are giving him a part of our concern. And when a man robs us, he is taking more than gold. He is depriving us of a part of ourselves, and this is what disturbs and upsets us.

We are interested in enforcing this commandment largely out of a desire to protect our own property, but God's concern is for something else. God understands that a man's life does not consist in the things which he possesses, that prestige based on the acquisition of goods is phony. Such a person does not in fact own anything. He is possessed by his possessions, so that if they should be taken from him, he himself would evaporate. This commandment appears to be less concerned for the robbed than for the robber.

I have tried to imagine what it is in a person which would compel him to steal from someone else. I must confess that I would be afraid to break into someone's home. Maybe this is part of the explantation. Only a person who needs very badly to prove how unafraid he is, either to himself or to someone else, would be able to overcome such fear. This would have to be someone who has turned against society and who feels that society has turned against him. What better way to get revenge than by making off with that which society values most highly, its material possessions. Victor Hugo in *Les Miserables* has shown how stealing depends on the anger of the robbed. All that is needed to destroy a theft is to give the robber what he is trying to take. The kindly old priest gives his candlesticks to Jean Valjean and so makes it impossible for him to take them.

We would imagine at first thought that stealing would be more common during hard times when there were many poor people living a hand-to-mouth existence. But this is not true at all. If it were, stealing ought to be less common now than it was during the depression, when it fact it is increasing all the time. The classic myth of robbery is Robin Hood who is said to have stolen from the rich in order to give to the poor. However noble and appealing such mythology sounds, in whatever form it may appear, it remains impossibly unreal. Stealing is a visible form of hatred. It is done to avenge one's self on the rich and to become one of them. A man who must steal to reinforce his own existence is incapable of giving to someone else. I cannot imagine that many stolen goods end up in church offering plates, or the robbers are inclined to be generous. Stealing hurts the robber far more than it does the robbed, for he acquires something for which he has not paid, something which he has sought to possess without investing any of himself. His goods are not and cannot be a part of himself. Thus his giving, if it should occur, could not be an expression of love.

One of the first signs that a man is on his way toward a healthy life with God is that he is able to part freely and even willingly with his material goods. One of the first danger signals in our life with God is when our giving no longer gives us joy and satisfaction. At the point of our possessions we either shrivel up into hoarders and misers of gadgets or are made larger by what we own. And our attitude toward other people's possessions says a great deal about our attitude toward them and toward the God who made them and gave them what they have. The man who must steal is the man who believes that he is trapped in a loveless world, a world in which there is no one to care for him, a world in which he must fend for himself in any way he can.

The deepest theft of all then is the claim that we are our own. We have been purchased by God at so fantastic a price that we cannot begin to measure our value.

The seventh command frees us from all self-directed materialism to attend to those essentials of life which cannot be stolen but only received, and which can be enjoyed only when they are given away again. That it is better to give than to receive is not a pious fiction; it is an observable reality. The truly rich are not those who keep but those who give. Stealing is a visible form of hatred, as giving is a visible form of love. God so loved that he gave. And so God is in all giving. A cup of water given in his name, a coat, a dress, a pair of shoes, a dollar bill—God is in such transactions. His presence cannot be detected by any Dow-Jones average, but he has assured us that as we do it for the least of these his brethren, we do it for him. This commandment is our promise of a cup so filled to overflowing that we will need never to take our neighbor's cup, but will have always enough to fill both his cup and our own.

9

To Tell the Truth

"You shall not bear false witness against your neighbor."
—*Exodus 20:16*

One of the most revolutionary things about Christianity is God's determination to let people in on what he is doing. In the first centuries of the church newspapers would have been unthinkable, not simply because the printing press had not yet been invented, but also because no one thought it was particularly necessary for people to be told anything. Decisions were made by a small handful of men who cared nothing about the will of their people. The less people knew about what was going on in the world, the better their government got along. But God felt otherwise. He thought it was essential that people should be told the news, and he went to great lengths to let them in on it, even to the extent of sending his own personal representatives.

There were, in those days, two ways by which people might communicate with each other over long distances. One was by sending a letter, a slow and somewhat uncertain method. The average person could expect to send and receive only a handful of letters in a lifetime.

When he wrote, he would sit down and carefully compose his letter, and when he received one, he would save it so that he might read and reread it to himself and to his friends. This is the origin of a great part of the New Testament. The epistles are letters which people sent from one church to another, letters which were preserved and which finally found their way into the Bible.

The other way of communicating over long distances was by sending a special messenger. Sometimes these messengers traveled on foot, walking and running— walking and running in the ancient pattern which our Boy Scouts still learn as the scout pace. If a city were down in the valley, as many cities were in the ancient world, these messengers might be visible for many miles as they came down out of the mountains, giving poignant meaning to Isaiah's word: "How beautiful upon the mountain are the feet of him who brings good news."

The Greek word for messenger is *aggelos.* And the message which he brings is that which comes from an angel, or *euaggelion.* In English this word becomes *goodspell,* or good news, shortened now to become our word *gospel.* The evangel has found its way into our vocabulary in such words as *evangelism, evangelist,* and *evangelical.* Buried in each of these words is the angel, the messenger. Anyone who speaks for God, who brings good news from God to man, is such a messenger.

Thus communication between God and man cannot be separated from communication between man and man.

No communication is possible without some common ground of truth, and where such common ground exists, the truth will out, communication will take place even without words, perhaps sometimes in spite of words. God's concern in this commandment is to preserve the integrity of human communication. He has everything at stake in this. Where communication between people has broken down through suspicion and distrust, there God has lost an essential avenue of approach to man. Of course, the opposite is also true. Where communication with God has broken down, there men have lost the common ground which makes communication with each other possible, and eventually they will discover that they are speaking different languages. This commandment, like the second, is concerned about that miracle by which two personalities reveal and exchange heart and mind with one another.

This command is set within a legal context. It calls to mind a courtroom and a witness stand. The trial is almost over. All the evidence has been heard. There is no jury, even though the defendant has been charged with a crime which carries a mandatory sentence of death. All the evidence has gone against the accused, but no one in the courtroom believes him to be guilty. In spite of this, it is obvious to everyone that he will be convicted. We know the ending of this story well. The judge goes out to the noisy crowds which are demanding the death sentence and melodramatically washes his hands as if he might thereby escape responsibility for the safety of a man he has found to be innocent. And the crowds, in a burst of truth greater than they know, cry out, "His blood be on us and on our children."

What a confused, contradictory scene. The accused becomes the witness. "For this was I born," he said, "and for this I have come into the world, to bear witness to the truth." And the judge turned out to be the one on trial. Pilate understood only too well that his own future was at stake. If word reached Rome that he could not handle these troublesome Jews, he might be transferred, and his career as a public servant put in jeopardy. Why should he risk his own position for the sake of an unknown street preacher whom he would never see again? The world, he thought, had such need of Pilate that it could easily dispense with Jesus. As things turned out, we must now refer to Pilate every time we confess our faith, when otherwise we might never have heard of him.

It was in this little courtroom dialog that Pilate asked his classic question, "What is truth?" Pilate knew well enough what was true, but this did not enable him to relate himself to Christ. Christianity does not present us with a tidy set of doctrines to be memorized and digested. Being Christian is more than knowing the right answers, not because Christianity has no answers, but because Christian answers cannot be separated from Christian witnesses. Here religion differs from science. Science deals with a kind of truth which is independent of its bearer, but religion has to do with that truth which is not true until it becomes true for its bearer.

The communication of religious truth presupposes an embodiment of truth in its bearer; it requires a relationship of concern and trust between its bearer and its hearer. When this relationship is present communication will take place which is profounder than any mere exchange of words. Every vision of God when it is reduced to words seems flat and tame. To relate the vision one must first enter into it.

In court or out of court we are all witnesses whether we wish to be or not. It will always be easier, I suppose, for us to see the evil in another than to see it in ourselves. This is why justice must be tempered with love. This commandment requires that we learn to look for all that is good in our neighbor. Just as every man is to be considered innocent until he is proven guilty, so each man is entitled to be regarded well until he is proven otherwise. In actual practice, someone has to believe a person guilty before he can gather the evidence on which he can be brought to trial. So sometimes we will have to speak the awful truth—but only out of love desiring to protect others from evil, not out of revenge and vindictiveness.

When a woman asks her husband, "How do you like my new hat?" she is not asking for the truth, and no husband would be so foolish as to tell it to her. All communciation which is born of love contains statements which could not be proved in a laboratory or a courtroom but which are truth in the deepest sense of the word. Every young man marries the most wonderful girl in the world, and every child's mother is the most beautiful woman in the world. Now and again there will be those who imagine themselves to be above this kind of foolishness, who pride themselves on their brutal honesty in every situation. One is supposed always to know where he stands with such a person. In point of fact, such people quite often turn out to be rather sensitive about this candid frankness when it is directed against themselves. Truth has become for them a kind of weapon by which they defend themselves through constant offense. This is the exact opposite of honesty. Truth which communicates personally can only be spoken in love. Where it is spoken out of any other motive, however factual it may be, it is not truth.

Self-interest inevitably colors human communication. If this is true for individuals, it is, if anythng, even more true for nations. Propaganda has been developed to a fine art. Public opinion can be molded and shaped to a frightening degree by public relations, so that even newspapers have become the victims of managed news, and are being used inadvertently to give shape to history by pulling public opinion in one direction or another. If a country is to be guided by the will of the people, the people must have the facts necessary for making an informed and intelligent decision. The importance of the news can hardly be overestimated. But if the sources of the news have come under the control of special interests, so that the newspapers receive only what someone decides they ought to know, no matter how accurate this information is it will present an incomplete and therefore distorted picture of reality. This would be disastrous to a democracy and must not be tolerated. Perhaps to some extent the newspapers are themselves to blame, having been content for too long to live on prepared news releases rather than going out after news on their own.

All propaganda is ultimately self-defeating, as advertisers are beginning to discover. When people begin to consider and discount the source of truth, effective communication will soon break down. Patriotism is not enhanced by a tendency to hide or excuse the evils of our own country, while exposing and exaggerating the evils of another. The cold war is a war of words in which truth has become the greatest victim. This is as true when we blame ourselves too much for failures over which we had no real control as when we take too much credit for victories in which many others also have had a part. Neither the United States nor Russia could have made their dramatic breakthroughs in nuclear physics without the help of German scientists. The race for the moon does not really prove anything significant about the relative merits or quality of our respective systems. The only valid measure of an educational system is its ability to produce well-educated people. An open system is so far superior to one which is closed that we need to be more concerned than we are about our openness to truth from whatever source it may come. What a tragedy it would be if we were forced into a position where we must say that black is white simply because communists are saying it is black.

A related issue is censorship in any form. Every gen-

eration produces enough bad literature to make an effective case for censorship. But this turns out always to be
a cure worse than the evil it is designed to correct.
Every freedom is capable of being abused, but because
freedoms are sometimes misused is no reason for abolishing them. The Fifth Amendment, for example, has come
to be almost synonymous with criminal conspiracy, but
this is not sufficient reason for removing it from our
Bill of Rights. For all that it has been badly abused,
this is still a very important protection for us all, one
without which we would all be poorer. As with capital
punishment, better that ten guilty people should escape
punishment by resorting to the Fifth Amendment than
that one innocent person should be punished for lack
of it. So too with censorship. Once the principle has
been established that one human being is entitled to
decide what other human beings may read and what
they ought not to read, the doors of tyranny have been
opened. But so long as the truth is free, there freedom
cannot be extinguished.

Luther has a marvelous phrase in which he says concerning our neighbor that we must "speak well of him,
apologize for him, and put the most charitable construc-
tion on all that he does." In these days of keen competition, when careers can be ruined overnight, we are much
more apt to look for the chinks in our neighbor's armor
than to try to cover up for him. Love does not delight
in exposing evil. The open frankness of what passes for
realism in much contemporary literature, and more
recently in contemporary films, does not grow out of

concern for truth and honesty, but out of an effort to expose humanity to pitiless and cynical scrutiny for selfish, financial advantage, a kind of literary voyeurism for profit. As Christians we have an obligation to understand our neighbor, and frankness is seldom understanding. Lack of such understanding will lead inevitably to a witness which is false.

What we speak is, in a curious way, an extension of ourselves. Ultimately all real communication is a sharing between two personalities. What we are is a part of our witness. When a Christian is afraid he reveals to his neighbor that his God is inadequate. When a Christian is unjust he reveals to his neighbor that his God is unconcerned. When a Christian is selfish he reveals to his neighbor that his God belongs only to him. This too is a false witness directed toward our neighbor.

The health of our own life with God cannot be separated from our concern for our neighbor's spiritual well being. How much difference does it make to us whether or not he knows and loves God? Just here is where our lives acquire a fourth dimension. We become the spokesmen, the witnesses, the ambassadors for Christ. Whether in the context of a scheduled, structured program of evangelism or in spontaneous, casual conversation, at a crucial point in someone's life we speak for God. It may well be that from the point of view of eternity this will be the most important single event in our life. "For this cause I came into the world, and for this reason was I born, that I might bear witness to the truth." No doubt it will sometimes seem like pure presumption that a man should claim to speak for God. And so it would be were it not for the promise of this eighth commandment.

If we are not to be false witnesses, it must be that we can and will bear a true witness to our neighbor. As I stand before the altar leading my congregation in worship I sometimes ask myself, "Who do you think you are that you should presume to speak for God?" Then it is that I must fall back on the promise of this command. In spite of our faults, in spite of our shortcomings, where love is present, the truth will out, the message will come through. You shall not bear a false witness to your neighbor, but you will and must bring him the truth.

10

King of the Mountain

"You shall not covet your neighbor's house; . . ."
—*Exodus 20:17a*

The Ten Commandments can be numbered in two different ways. Roman Catholics and Lutherans make one command out of the opening section of the Decalogue which deals with other gods, while most Protestants divide these verses into two separate commands, one forbidding other gods and the other prohibiting graven images. Thus, what is the second command for a Lutheran will be the third command for a Presbyterian. And at the end of the Decalogue, Protestants make a single command of the section regarding coveting, while Lutherans and Roman Catholics see this as two separate commands, the ninth having to do with covetous feelings toward our neighbor's house, and the tenth relating to an unholy desire for our neighbor's possessions. Hebrew scholars are also divided over the proper numbering of the commandments, although in practice most Jews follow the Protestant numbering.

This variation in numbering the commandments is not exactly an earth-shaking difference of opinion,

although heaven knows Christians have split apart over
questions more trivial than this. Yet, since so large a
part of Christendom distinguishes between two kinds
of coveting, there must be some rationale behind this
way of numbering the commands. The difference between the ninth and tenth commandments need not be
glossed over, as tempting as it is to speak of these two
kinds of desire as if they were the same. The ninth command has to do with our attitude toward the place
where our neighbor lives, while the tenth command concerns itself with the things which our neighbor owns.
A house is to give us space in which to live, while possessions provide us with the means for living. To wish
to occupy the space in which our neighbor lives is to
lust for power over him. The ninth command thus ad-
dresses itself to that hunger for power which is so
much a part of human life.

The world cannot be divided up into little patches
of ground, one patch to a person, with each person
living out his life totally within his own little patch.
Inevitably his life collides with other lives. He must
occupy the place in which his neighbor also stands, and
just there the struggle for power begins. We assert ourselves and our neighbor is affected.

Sometimes children play a symbolic game called "King
of the Mountain." The goal is to start at the bottom of
the heap and work your way up by pushing down everyone ahead of you until finally you have knocked off the
top man, and there you stand, the King of the Mountain. In their innocent little game our children act out

one of the most basic and inescapable facts of life. The drive for power takes many forms and has many names, but in the end it comes to the same thing—a desire, a need, a hunger to stand where our neighbor stands, to elbow him out of the way, discreetly if possible, roughly if necessary, so that we can occupy his place. Competition is a basic element of life. What helps us get ahead seems good, what holds us back is bad. While we pay lip service to good sportsmanship, ("It's not whether you win or lose, but how you play the game") our heart isn't in it. Deep down we know that what really counts is who wins, and no one asks how he did it. All the world loves a winner, for a while at least; and all the world would like to be a winner.

This subtle drive for power creeps in everywhere. Certainly it is no stranger in the church. The level of conversation among the disciples during the Last Supper is indicated by this little note: "a dispute arose among them, which of them was to be regarded as the greatest." The proud reluctance of the Pharisees to share their priceless knowledge of God with the Gentile world, the impressive power of the medieval church which could make and unmake kings and empires, the sophisticated rivalry which goes on nowadays between denominations and congregations and pastors—the history of the church is pock-marked with the scars of an unholy lust for power.

The history of humanity too is strewn with the wreckage left behind by would-be conquerors who dreamed of ruling the world. But the ultimate failure of these kingdom seekers never seems to serve as a lesson for those who come after them. How many men alive today would not gladly become King of the Mountain if they had the chance? The lust for power is a driving force for more people than is comfortable to contemplate. So it is that nation is pitted against nation, region against region, state against state, town against town, neighborhood against neighborhood. "This turf belongs to the Purple Dragons," announces a boyish scrawl on the side of a building. And a member of the Hooded Knights may even have to pay with his life to discover who is in charge there. In the world of business it's a dog-eat-dog world, we say; though to be fair to our canine friends, they are seldom seen to devour one another as eagerly as do human beings. But we know all too well what is meant; the drive to get ahead, to compete, produces a world in which success determines morals. Anything that works is good; anything that brings failure is bad. The only real evil is getting caught. Even within households there is often a struggle for power, an unconscious rivalry for domination or for the affection of the children. Over and over the pattern is the same: one human being asserting himself at the expense of another.

What is the meaning of this need for power? Perhaps it rises out of a kind of insecurity about the place where we stand, and an illusion about the place where our neighbor stands. People who live in housing developments often joke about getting into the wrong house by mistake but in fact this almost never happens. Our own house speaks to us in a way quite different from any other on the block. It tells us that the lawn needs raking, the windows are not too clean, there is a shingle loose which will have to be repaired one of these days, the mortgage is not paid, and if the family gets any bigger there will have to be another room. When we look at our own house we see so many problems no one else can see. As for our neighbor's house, we see only a quiet, charming place which appeals to us. How could we know about the burdens, the secret sorrows which are underneath that roof? His house seems so desirable and ours so unsatisfactory.

No doubt all of us have known the quiet person who was so sure of himself, so confident of his own ability and position that he was somehow self-contained and had no need to prove his power to himself or to anyone else. I cannot help but think that our Lord must have been such a person. Because Jesus really was the King of the Mountain. He was the Lord of lords and the King of kings. He didn't have to prove anything about his power and he was in no doubt of the place in which he stood. He could let himself be arrested and led off to jail like any common criminal—and his pre-eminence was lessened not a whit.

Yet, if Jesus really was the King of the Mountain, why didn't he assert himself? Judas Iscariot for one had counted on that. But no, he let them get away with pushing him around. "As a lamb before its shearers is dumb, so he opened not his mouth." This is the exact opposite of competition, the reverse of a lust for power.

And this is the theme which runs through the whole of Jesus' ministry. "The meek shall inherit the earth." "He that exalts himself shall be humbled, and he that humbles himself shall be exalted." "He who lives by the sword shall also die by the sword." And perhaps the hardest word of all, "If anyone strikes you on the right cheek, turn to him the other also." Here we meet a non-aggression in Jesus which seems so alien to all we associate with power. A cartoon which appeared in the *New Yorker* magazine pictured a pompous and obviously powerful man sitting in church beside his well dressed wife exclaiming, "And I say the meek will *not* inherit the earth!" The whole idea of humility seems somehow so unrealistic and naive; there is something not quite masculine about it; people who turn the other cheek are apt to be sissies. In any case religion seems to be intent on holding people back from their drive for power, and is therefore not to be taken seriously.

Just here, if we could only see it, we are close to the heart of our life with God. A drive for power *is* a desire to stand where our neighbor stands, and paradoxically this is precisely what our faith requires of us. But there is a difference. What else does the Golden Rule mean than that we are to exchange places with our neighbor, that is, that we must deal with him as though we stood where he stands? Our Lord has not so much removed aggression and drive from human life as he has transformed them. We are no longer to be governed by a lust for power which seeks to dominate other people. Instead we are to be governed by concern for our neighbor's need. We put ourselves in his place not in order to drive him out of it but that it may be more securely his own.

Here is the deepest meaning of our Lord's own life. For in the truest sense he stands where we stand: he weeps with our tears, he shoulders our burdens, he trembles with our fears, and cowers under our doubts. He bows his head at the last so that he may die our death. "Do unto others as you would have others do unto you." What is it that God wants us to do for him? Well, what has he done for us? He has come to be with us where we are. And so he must want us to come and be with him where he is.

Here is the desire which God longs to see in us, a hunger for his house rather than for our neighbor's. "Lord, thou hast been our dwelling place in all generations." "How lovely is thy dwelling place, O Lord of hosts! My soul longs, yea, faints for the courts of the Lord." Here is a hunger, a drive which transforms life and redeems its powers. Rather than making us play at being little gods and so driving our neighbor away from us, here is a desire which unites us with God and brings us close to one another. We need not covet our neighbor's house because with all our heart we may long for God's house. This is implicit in God's promise to receive us into his eternal habitation.

This desire is exactly the dimension so often missing in what passes for life. How commonly we forget the most important fact of our existence: that we are eternal. This is the tragedy for those who covet their neighbor's

house. Their eyes are still glued on this world, their
hearts are still trapped in time. What a tiny ambition
it is after all to settle for our neighbor's house when we
might have God's for the asking. How calmly we can
move through life when our hearts are fixed on heaven,
how confident and self-contained we might then become, how strong we would be, and how much we could
suffer without crying out in pain or in imagined injustice. This is not the opiate of a religion which promises us pie in the sky by and by. This is the wide-eyed
courage of those who see reality in all its potentialities
and possibilities, and so are willing and able to suffer,
to permit God to have his way. This is a test of strength
greater than any rough and tumble contest of muscles
or missiles.

More to the point, here is a strength which permits us
to look again at the place where our neighbor really
lives. Who is our neighbor after all? The fellow next
door, to be sure. To get along with him may very well
be the acid test of our Christian love. But we must know
by now that our love can never stop there. We have
neighbors in some pretty unlikely and unenviable places,
places we could not covet for all the tea in China. With
a place of our own already prepared for us, we are free,
if we could only know it, to do something daring and
creative about some of the places our neighbors have to
live. For Christians there are no foreigners, no out-
siders, no "our-kind" and "their-kind." The battle for
decent housing is the great new moral frontier of our
civilization. The changing of these patterns will require

quiet courage and great strength. This is no job for sissies. The slums are still too profitable and the suburbs still too cozy to change easily. But this is what this commandment requires of us; that we stand where our neighbor stands and see the world through his eyes, and then act for him. For even now God has come to be with us where we are and has promised to stay with us always, even to the end of the age.

11

Be Glad You're You

"You shall not covet your neighbor's wife, or his man servant, or his maid servant, or his ox, or his ass, or anything that is your neighbor's."
—*Exodus 20:17b*

Henrik Ibsen in his play *Peer Gynt* has drawn a perfect portrait of a discontented man. Peer is first seen as a charming, attractive, immensely talented young man who is completely unable to settle down to the life of a Norwegian farmer. He cannot be satisfied with the family estate which has fallen to him, nor with the sweet and lovely Solveig, his childhood sweetheart. Leaving his friends behind, he sets out to explore the world and to carve a niche in it for himself. The play follows him through many lands and adventures, and we are permitted to see him win and lose several fortunes. Finally, at the end of the play, Peer finds himself back in the mountains of Norway near the old family farm. He is much older now, but little wiser and greatly disillusioned.

There he falls into a deep sleep and in a dream encounters a remarkable person who calls himself the Button Molder. The Button Molder's task it seems is to wander about the world in search of lost souls. He has been commissioned by the Creator, he says, to melt down these souls again and to remold them as a button molder might remake old buttons. Peer is distressed to learn that the Button Molder has been looking for him. When he protests, the Button Molder replies, "The Master, you see, is economical. He never throws away as useless a single thing that may be dealt with as raw material. Now, you were meant to be a gleaming button on the world's waistcoat, but your loop was missing, so you've got to go back into the scrap heap to be melted fresh again."

Naturally Peer objects to this proposal, to which the Button Molder answers, "But my dear Peer, there is no need for you to make so great a fuss about so small a thing; because you have never yet been yourself. What difference can it make to you, if, when you die, you disappear?" Peer had so much that should have made him happy. But he died the unhappiest of men. To be so discontented with one's lot in life is, as Ibsen saw, to throw some doubt on the wisdom of the Creator who made us what we are. It is to wish to be remade after some other image of our own devising.

How often it happens that we find ourselves wishing we might change places with someone else. We set our hearts on goals which someone else has already reached, and then torture ourselves with the knowledge that they have what we can only long for. Seldom do we stop to ask whether our goal can ever be the same as that of someone else, or whether, if we should reach it, we would be happy with it. We are so sure that if only we were as strong and athletic, as talented and beautiful, as intelligent and capable as someone else, we would then be happy and content. We are certain that success must be as sweet as its smell, that riches are as rewarding as the lack of them is depressing.

We live in a world which sets great store by material possessions. This is nothing new. Sometimes people talk as if materialism were an invention of the twentieth century. As long ago as the time of Moses human happiness was made to depend on the acquisition and accumulation of things. Even then people tended to compare themselves with one another, to measure their own success in life by the attainment of someone else, to make themselves miserable because of another's good fortune. It is this tendency toward comparison to which this commandment speaks.

We can hardly avoid a certain concern for material things. To speak as if the man of God could somehow exist without his daily bread is nonsense. Things come from God and are his gifts to us for our use in making life easier and more rewarding. It is not money, but the unholy love of money, which is the root of evil. Very few people love money for its own sake. Only a demented miser here and there actually enjoys the mere accumulation of gold and the satisfaction of counting it and hiding it away. Most of us love money for what it means and for what it can do for us. Money is a means of transaction, a medium of exchange. It represents our labor or our ingenuity. When we trade it for something else, we are giving a part of ourselves in exchange for something we need or want. Possessions become, in this sense, an enlargement of ourselves.

But something more than this is at work. How does it happen that we not only long for possessions, but for more possessions than our neighbor has? Clearly we are hoping to prove something to ourselves and perhaps to him. Material success seems to indicate that fortune has smiled on us, that our existence has somehow been vindicated and authenticated by our good fortune. Failure, on the other hand, seems to suggest that our existence is in doubt, that we are being punished by the fates for some shortcoming, most likely one for which we are not responsible. Oh, the injustice of it all! The ancient Jew was not alone in imagining that riches were an evidence of God's blessing and that poverty was divine punishment. Modern man may not put it in quite so theological a fashion, but it comes to the same thing. The rich man is the good man; the poor man is somehow reprehensible. To move from poverty to riches is to demonstrate that one is not guilty after all, that he is as good as the richest of men.

But such progress from poverty to riches is difficult at best. It requires a combination of talent and good luck which very few people achieve. The rags to riches story appears and reappears in the mythology of every generation as the classic expression of the human dream. But it remains a myth precisely because it happens so rarely in reality. Since few men can actually hope to achieve this kind of self-justification, we must settle for the next best thing. If we cannot reach up to the rich man's level, then we can pull him down to our own, and perhaps succeed in getting him lower than ourselves. This is why no one really loves a truly wealthy man any more than a truly good one. The possession of great riches is in itself a guarantee of jealous, covetous envy. No one believes that rich men have attained their wealth honestly. There is always the unspoken suspicion that he must have done something unspeakably unscrupulous to have gotten so rich. So we have the irony by which people both envy and suspect great riches.

There can be little doubt that this kind of envy and suspicion lies behind much of the bad feeling which Americans seem to generate wherever they go. Our best motives are suspected, and our generosity is met with scorn. This is not because we are really all that rich. We seldom think of ourselves as wealthy or even well off. By comparison, however, we are surely fabulously rich alongside a Chinese coolie or an African native. It is precisely this disparity in wealth for which neither the rich nor the poor is responsible which has given rise to much of the tension between nations, and which accounts for the attractiveness of communism. In its crudest form, communism is a promise to level off these disparities, to reward each man equally so that no one will be able to lord it over another, or seem to have been more especially blessed than another. On the face of it, the Communist appears to be motivated by the most humanitarian of concerns. But in fact he is quite as badly caught in the trap of envy and covetousness as any dirty capitalist. For at the same moment that the Communist speaks of equality he speaks also of improvement and progress; he exchanges one man's dream of vast riches for society's eventual wealth as the result of an endless series of Five and Ten Year plans.

In neither case is there much hope for satisfaction or contentment; and this dissatisfaction is what this commandment is speaking to. St. Paul once wrote: "Not that I complain of want; for I have learned, in whatever state I am, to be content." There is, to be sure, a vast difference between this Christian contentment, and that apathy which is a kind of despair. Contentment suggests too often nothing more inspiring than a herd of cattle. Such lethargy does not seem worthy of mention among the Christian virtues. We have known too many people whose contentment with life was a form of giving up in which nothing needed to be changed because nothing was of any use anymore. Christian contentment surely cannot mean that we are to be satisfied with the world as it is. This is pure complacency for which there is no room in the Christian scheme of things. There is to be rather, a "divine discontent" which will not permit things to remain as they are, but is always hopeful of making them better and happier than they are.

The discontent which motivated Paul did not prevent him from being content with himself and his own lot in life. With all the riches of the kingdom of God as his own possession, what use could he have had for the status symbols of temporal affluence? He could be content precisely because he had no more need to compare himself with someone else. He had no need to look with jaundiced eyes on the success of someone else and covet it for his own. He had found a life so meaningful that he would not have traded it for any other in the world. He was able in the truest sense to be glad to be what he was. "By the grace of God, I am what I am," he wrote. He was glad to be himself.

This command, therefore, does not concern itself so much with possessions or the lack of them as it does with the meaning of possessions. Sometimes it is aimed at poor people to keep them contented in their poverty and to prevent them from being envious of their wealthy neighbors. But this commandment in no way suggests that poverty is good or that wealth is bad. Nor does it indicate that it is wrong for a man to long for more of this world's goods than he now possesses. As always, God is more concerned about *why* we do what we do than he is for *what* we do. He is interested not so much in whether we want more than we have, but why we want it. What is it that we think new wealth might bring us which we do not now possess?

We could not learn to hate what we are and have if we did not know what we might have been, that we could have been someone else, that we could have had what they possess. It is the comparison which hurts, and comparison is the key which unlocks this commandment. It speaks to that tendency of ours to keep one eye always on someone else, to measure ourselves not as we are in ourselves, but as we stack up against somebody else.

Coveting is the most secret of all sins. It may sometimes come to light when one of the commandments is broken; but more often it stays buried deep within us, smoldering away, creating dissatisfaction, hatred, and envy which eat away at our contentedness and make us hate someone for his good fortune and feel sorry for ourselves when our own seems to be less than his. We must work so hard for all that we get, while everything seems to come so easily to him. We despise him for his success, his good looks, his intelligence, his athletic prowess, his popularity, his money, his car, and his home.

Of course, such envy makes it impossible for us to see our neighbor's need. We are so sure of his affluence and of our own poverty that it never occurs to us to look for the holes in his shoes or the worn places on his coat which give the lie to his apparent success. Seldom does it dawn on us that he is trying just as hard as we are to keep up an appearance of prosperity, that he is as proud as we of what he has made of his life, and as reluctant as we to admit that he may be having a hard time of it. We wear such genial masks that we rarely really talk to one another.

The advertisers know perfectly well how to set us off on a binge of self-pity which can be quieted only by the acquisition of still another gadget. Our generation could easily become known as the gadget generation. Perhaps nothing else so well explains the incredible popularity of trading stamps. What could be more exciting than the possibility of adding to one's collection of gadgets? The more gadgets one possesses, the more prosperous he appears to be. Here, if anywhere, we are responsible ourselves for the disquieting legacy of hatred which is coming back to haunt us as Americans. For it is we, by and large, who have taught the world to believe that the worth of a nation lies in the quality and quantity of its gadgets; it is we who have sold the notion that the way to the good life is to acquire and accumulate more and more trinkets. Having created in others desires which they cannot possibly fulfill, we ought not be surprised if they turn their frustrated envy against the creators of those desires.

We consistently present to the world and even to ourselves an image of the American way of life which is so closely associated with the possession of the outward symbols of wealth and success that the difference is not always visible to the naked eye. The goal of the good life as encouraged by television presents our children and our young people with a questionable standard of values to which to commit themselves. Since we insist on describing the good life in such lavish terms, we ought not be surprised if so many young people, unable to attain their dream in any other way, take the shortest and most obvious way by turning to dissolution or crime. With our ears we hear that crime does not pay. But our eyes see another story.

The world indeed has needs and hungers which no amount of material possessions can satisfy. "Why do you spend your money for that which is not bread, and your labor for that which does not satisfy?" Isaiah asked. This is the tragedy of coveting. It leaves one as dissatisfied when it is fulfilled as he was before. Ibsen saw that such discontent is in fact a kind of rebuke against the Creator who has made us what we are. This commandment contains within it a promise from that same Creator to provide us with all we need to make life rich and meaningful, so that we may be glad to be ourselves. And a part of that reward will be our creative concern for our neighbor's need by which we can be genuinely glad for another's achievements and truly pleased by anyone's good fortune.

12

Command Performance

*"I am the good shepherd. The good shepherd lays
down his life for the sheep. He who is a hireling and
not a shepherd, whose own the sheep are not, sees
the wolf coming and leaves the sheep and flees; and
the wolf snatches them and scatters them. He flees
because he is a hireling and cares nothing for the
sheep. I am the good shepherd; I know my own and
my own know me, as the Father knows me and I
know the Father; and I lay down my life for the
sheep. And I have other sheep, that are not of this
fold; I must bring them also, and they will heed my
voice. So there shall be one flock, one shepherd. For
this reason the Father loves me, because I lay down
my life, that I may take it again.*

—John 10:11-17

The Gospel of John does not contain any parables. But
it has at least one extended metaphor which might easily
have been a parable in its original form. It begins with
the words, "I am the Good Shepherd," and it has all the
elements of a story. There is a setting: a pasture and a
sheepfold. There is a cast of characters: sheep and a

shepherd, a hired man and a wolf. And reading somewhat between the lines, there is a rather exciting plot.
The terrified sheep can smell the wolf long before the
hired hand senses any danger. The shepherd would have
known—he would have recognized a certain restlessness
within the flock. But the hired man is unaware, his concern is somewhere else. Then there is a sudden rush of
running sheep and their frightened, helpless cries as the
wolf springs out from the underbrush. The hireling
hesitates, trying to decide whether to go after the wolf
or to run for the shepherd. Then, concluding that dis-
cretion is the better part of valor, he runs off to fetch
the shepherd. We see the shepherd hurrying out to chase
off the wolf and rescue his sheep. To make certain all
the sheep are safe and accounted for, he calls them together from their hiding places in the grass. Such is their
confidence in him that the sheep reappear at the sound
of their shepherd's voice. Leading them back to the fold,
the shepherd counts them as they pass through the nar-
row little door, and then when he is satisfied that they
are all secure he lies down in the gateway, prepared to
spend the night there in case the wolf should come back
again.

Only one of the characters in this story is identified.
Jesus says that he is the shepherd. What is more, he
claims to be a *good* shepherd. And from his parable we
can understand what Jesus meant by goodness. Clearly
he does not mean by good the opposite of bad. If this
were so he would have contrasted himself with the wolf,
who is the villain of the story. It is the wolf who is evil,

who comes to steal, to kill and to destroy. If to steal and kill and destroy makes someone bad, then not to steal or kill or destroy ought to make him good. But the hired man did none of these things and still he does not qualify as good. He was frightened but this hardly makes him evil. He ran away for the simple reason that the sheep did not belong to him. He had no good reason for staying. The sheep were not his own, and he could hardly be expected to risk his life for them.

The shepherd, on the other hand, placed his own life between the sheep and the wolf not because he was not afraid but because the sheep belonged to him. In a curious way which he could not have explained so as to make sense to anyone else, the sheep were a part of him. His life and theirs were all bound up together. The shepherd was good because he was faithful. When the chips were down he did not throw in his hand. He met life head-on.

Sometimes it is said that faith makes life easier. It is supposed to give a person peace of mind, to cure diseases, even to make plants grow faster. But in this story, exactly the opposite was the case. It was the hired hand, the unfaithful one, who had an easy time of it. He just ran off when the going got rough. It was the faithful one who had to stand his ground and meet the danger. Far from making his life easier, faith made his life more hazardous.

It is the faithful person who, precisely because of his faith, is prevented from taking the easy way out. When the Bible speaks of faith it is not referring to the things which a person believes to be true. Nor is it talking about a certain ability to make seemingly impossible things happen. Rather, it speaks of faithfulness, as in this word of Christ: "Because you have been faithful in a few things I will make you master over many things." The Christian has been given a certain trust to keep, a responsibility to discharge, a calling to fulfill, and his faith involves his faithfulness to this trust. In the last analysis, this faithfulness is possible only as a trust in the God who is himself faithful to those who belong to him.

The world will always try to talk the Christian out of such faithfulness. There is a certain irrationality to this kind of dogged faith which looks perverse and fanatical. The rational, logical thing to do is what the hired man did. Leave your post; why risk your neck? This is how the world thinks, and it makes good sense. But the man of faith is held, bound, tied, rooted to the spot to which he has been called, and his faith consists in this one idiotic thing: that no matter what happens he has to stand his ground. "Here I stand," cried Luther, "because there is nothing else I can do."

But see what happens when the shepherd stands his ground. The wolf is frightened off. The sheep are brought back together again. Order is brought back to what nearly became chaos. God is, after all, the God of order. When at creation he looked at the world and found it *good* he was not boasting about his own work. He was simply observing that where once there had been pure chaos, disorder, emptiness, there was now meaningful, purposeful order. Because order involves both time and space, it requires faithfulness. That the Creator is pleased with his creation implies that he means to stand by it. And stand by it he has. This is the whole story of the Bible and the whole history of God's people, the incredible, fantastic faithfulness of God.

And now he means once more to create us in his image. He has given each of us a calling, a sphere in which he asks us to be faithful, to hold our ground, to meet life head-on. He doesn't ask us to be talented, effective, or efficient. He only asks that we be faithful. But we learn to be so good at evading issues, at dodging the ball we were supposed to catch, that after awhile we are no longer aware there is a problem. The wolf is snapping away right and left and we are apt to be busily thinking that we have things well under control.

We hear on every side that the man who gets along in this world, after all, is the one who learns to compromise, to cut corners, to take the line of least resistance. This is how to succeed in business, or anywhere else, without really trying. Success is made of many things, but moral courage is seldom one of them. The person with guts, the one who is faithful, will have to say what he thinks, and this, of course, is all wrong. In this world one says what he is expected to say, what he thinks someone might like him to say. We become so used to this kind of nonsense that we can listen to TV commercials with a perfectly straight face. Of course, the advantage gained by those who cut corners is illusory. Their tragedy is not that they may not get away with their petty crimes (since many people seem never to get caught), nor that they contri-

bute to the degradation of their country or the downfall
of civilization. Their tragedy is that they are trapped
within the shell of their own smallness, their world is as
tiny as themselves, and with each new trespass it shrinks
in on them a little tighter. For anyone actually to prefer
this kind of imprisonment, this evasion of life, is surely
a sort of insanity.

This is exactly why faithful people, to say nothing of
a faithful God, are so uncomfortable to have around.
They have a way of calling into question the illusions
by which people live. They do this not because they
argue a lot and raise questions all the time, but just because they keep so everlastingly at their posts. By their
faithfulness the world will eventually be worn down and
required to listen to what they are saying and see what
they are doing. Suddenly the world will discover that
these are the only people who have been talking to the
point all along; these are the only ones who have come
to terms with the realities of life. The rest have been
content to skim off the surface, to beg the question, and
never quite to meet life head-on. One day the world will
wake up to discover that it is coming apart at the seams,
that the starch has come out of its religion, and then it
will demand that some kind of order be imposed on all
this chaos. But it's not that easy. We can't run off and
get the shepherd. We must stand here and take what's
coming, and either be engulfed or turn the tide.

But if we can't run off, neither can God. He is held
here by a bond of love which nothing in this world can
break. (1) God is the infinitely, completely faithful one

who makes himself constantly and utterly available to every man. (2) He answers eagerly at the slightest mention of his name. (3) He speaks to us at the point of our deepest need. (4) He gives continuity and direction to all created life, insuring its indestructibility. (5) He shares his own creativity, and so preserves and enriches all of life. (6) He breaks into our solitary loneliness, and by turning us outward, away from ourselves, enables us to relate ourselves to him and to each other on the deepest level of our existence. (7) He provides all the material, physical resources needed to make life full and rewarding. (8) He establishes the ground of truth by which communication is made possible between himself and all intelligent life. (9) He breaks into our world, into the very places where we live our lives, and so gives us entree into the world which is beyond. (10) He so fills our lives as to make us glad to be what he has made us. God cannot keep us at our post against our will; but because he cannot run, neither can we. We are prisoners of his love.

Sometimes people talk as if the way to be a Christian is to imitate Christ. But this is quite impossible. We have no way of knowing what Jesus might have done in any given situation of life in the twentieth century. This is really a romantic notion by which one imagines what Christ might have done and then sets about to imitate his own imagination. However convenient such a devise might be for justifying what one would have done anyway, it clearly will not do as a basis for Christian morality. However disciplined such a life may appear to be, such imitation turns out always to be sheer fantasy. Our Lord nowhere suggests that he aimed at creating a world full of carbon copies of himself.

All the same, when two people love each other very much they tend to become more and more alike. We have often been intrigued by the intuitive understanding between jazz musicians which makes it possible for them to improvise widely and individually. Somehow it all makes sense and comes out right. Part of our amazement rises out of our own need to have our music written out note for note and measure by measure with nothing left to chance. This is not to suggest that jazz is undisciplined. Actually it is the most rigidly disciplined of all musical expression. What gives meaning to the improvisation is the unwritten understanding between the musicians; the beat. Jazz is a creative act of faith, improvisation within the boundaries of felt rhythm. The jazz musician is in this sense a moral pioneer who dares to break out of the prescribed into an intuitively responsive dialog in which the link between him and his fellow musicians is not a written score but sheer faith.

Just so, the Ten Commandments are open-ended. They tell us what not to do. What we are to do they do not say. All genuine morality is improvised on the spot and is therefore justified not by its accuracy in reproducing a sterile code but by its faithfulness to the claims of love. There is no possible way of reducing to mere words the claims of love in their totality. But this is not to suggest that such morality is therefore undisciplined. Improvised morality is more rigidly disciplined than any formal code because it rests on faith. The man who demands to be told what to do is precisely the man who does not believe. He must be shown. And his performance will be a still-born reproduction of a sterile code. The moral pioneer can break out of such dull, uncreative conformity into the infinitely more demanding sensitivity of responsible love.

Very often the writers of the Gospels explain a particular event in Jesus' life by saying that he did this or that in order that the scripture might be fulfilled. They do not mean to suggest by this that Jesus carried out his mission in a certain fashion only because he was obligated to an Old Testament statement about the Messiah, the Son of man. Every incident in Jesus' ministry was called forth by the immediate and genuine needs of the people around him. But his response was so sensitive to the demands of love that when the scripture was laid down over the outline of his life the reproduction was exact. This did not happen by mere accident. Jesus had so learned to love the law that it had become his second nature. It was his backbone as he was its flesh.

The Ten Commandments do not bind us to themselves. They bind us to God and him to us in a choreography of faith. So closely is God bound up with us and we with him that if we fall, he falls, and if he stands, we too may stand. But God does stand and will to all eternity. And we stand now in his place—which means that if we stand, the world has hope of standing too.

And since the world is God's the world in all its fulness and beyond belongs to those who love the law, who have seen beneath its ancient lines a glowing face of such spendid love that they are blind to every other beauty and deaf to any other word than his in whom they live and move and have their being.